SCENES FROM THE PAST : 41 (PA

RAILWAYS ACRO

MID-CHESHIRE

KNUTSFORD - NORTHWICH - CHESTER
HELSBY, WINSFORD and MIDDLEWICH

Northwich, August 1955: Undoubtedly the most impressive trains at Northwich were the '8F' powered, 1000 ton limestone hoppers from the ICI quarries at Peak Forest. 'Garratts' were proposed in 1936, and 'half trains' with '4Fs' ran in 1937 before Heaton Mersey '8Fs', subshedded at Northwich, took over with 16 hopper loads in 1938. Northwich gained the workings in 1949 and ran these vacuum braked trains with real panache - passenger speeds were no problem! No. **48500** is blowing off promisingly as she gets away with a set of return empty hoppers, whilst a GC '04' stands in the shed yard. Behind the wagons in the goods yard is the signal protecting Manchester Road crossing on Salt Branch No. 3 - the scene of the fatal accident in 1908.

B E Morrison

ALAN WILKINSON

Near **Mouldsworth, August 27th 1958.** Trafford Park's Stanier 2-6-4 tank No **42628** emerges from Delamere Forest and comes briskly down the 1 in 90 towards Mouldsworth with a train for Chester.
T Lewis, courtesy N E Preedy

RAILS ACROSS MID-CHESHIRE - INTRODUCTION

As a railway enthusiast, I was fortunate indeed to grow up within easy reach of two such very different railways as the West Coast Main Line and the Chester route of the Cheshire Lines Commitee. The former was one of the busiest main lines in the country and had been since its pioneer opening in 1837, whilst the CLC bustled with heavy freight, efficiently and conscientiously handled by an enthusiastic staff still very much CLC orientated, twenty years after Nationalisation.

Vivid are my childhood memories of being willingly coerced to walk the three miles to Winsford station on Sunday afternoons to see the Up 'Royal Scot', of going to sleep on still summer evenings to the sound of the overnight sleepers pounding northwards across the fields, and of being frequently pacified with a couple of hours on Middlewich station. Here, neither "Porter Jim" Lycett nor my mother had any hope of chiding me homewards until No 41229 and 'The Dodger' had been to Northwich AND back! Entertainment also came from No. 44155 and the 'Crewe Goods' shunting their vividly painted Cerebos and Seddons salt vans, together with ICI's 'Covhops' and limestone wagons, and there was always a chance of a clandestine footplate trip on the 4F. From 1958 to 1964, I haunted the main line between Minshull Vernon and Winsford, and so can just remember it with its magnificent Stanier Pacifics, as an all steam railway. Modernisation was inevitable, but once the overhead wires and new stations arrived, the character of the line was irretrievably changed, never more so than on that fateful Saturday, 26th September 1964, when No. 46256 bowed out in such grand form as the last working 'Duchess' on the RCTS 'Scottish Lowlander'.

Almost too late, I then discovered the CLC where District Relief Signalman Albert Booth kindly introduced me to numerous signal boxes, railwaymen, and especially to those Northwich enginemen who generously allowed me to share their footplates under cover of darkness when I should have been studying for 'A' levels! Trains moved on the CLC and the Northwich '8F's were hustled around with an urgency which left no doubt that not all epic performances emanated from Crewe North! Hours of enjoyment were savoured watching train after train-especially the 'Hoppers'-storm out of the Down yard and up 'over the arches' to Hartford.

In these straightened times, the West Coast Route remains fairly busy although badly in need of the next phase of modernisation, but rationalisation at Northwich throughout the 'Eighties' has been severe. Product changes at ICI have seen some rail traffic transferred to Runcorn whilst transport policies hostile to Railfreight have seen the Up yard closed and the whole complex served by a relative handful of block workings. Regular freight traffic has ceased west of Hartford Junction, returning only temporarily with reversal at Chester as the price of putting the Hartford spur 'Out of Use' for eight months from August 1994.

Hence this book is essentially about the period up to the early 'Seventies. the emphasis is towards the CLC and also the LNWR branches since volumes have already been written elsewhere about the West Coast Main Line. Mid Cheshire does not appear to have been much visited by photographers before the 'Fifties, but if readers know of the existence of other sources of earlier material, particularly the Middlewich branch, I should be most grateful for further information.

The most recent scenes in this book were taken almost thirty years ago and reveal a railway scene changed almost beyond ecognition today. Modernisation and rationalisation have decimated the infrastructure and the railway communities which kept the traffic moving. It is difficult not to predict even further contraction as a consequence of the recent ill-conceived privatisation scheme imposed without reference to a coherant national transport policy. Record what there is for it may not be there tomorrow! This is what the railways of Mid Cheshire used to be like; they are unlikely to be quite so fascinating in the future.

Alan Wilkinson
Sutton Coldfield

A GRAND TRUNK ROUTE

Serving the Cheshire Saltfield was hardly a priority for the promoters of the first railway to cross the area: The Grand Junction Railway opened in July 1837, and was conceived as one of the first great main lines, linking the pioneering Liverpool and Manchester Railway of 1830 at Newton Le Willows with the London and Birmingham Railway which opened in 1838. The line was taken boldly across country, bridging the Weaver on two impressive viaducts and passing some one and a half miles to the west of Northwich. It would have passed close to Winsford but for the objections of the Salt owners on Wharton Common; the subsequent Over and Wharton branch ineffectually met the areas passenger needs, whilst the mainline station remained forever distant from the town. By 1847 the Grand Junction was part of the West Coast Route to Scotland and owned by the London and North Western Railway, the 'Premier Line', destined to become the most prosperous railway in the country.

(Below) **Knutsford West, c. 1949.** An LNER "J39" 0-6-0 heads a west-bound feight towards Northwich.

P. M. Alexander - Millbrook House Collection

SERVING THE SALTFIELD

Whilst the LNWR was empire building, establishing its renowned railway centre at Crewe in the eighteen forties, it rather neglected the saltfield and the first proposal for a line into the area came from the North Staffordshire Railway. The NSR had reached Ettiley Heath, Sandbach, in January 1852, and poor relations with the LNWR found it aiming for an independent route to Liverpool or Birkenhead via Middlewich and Northwich. In 1855, a firm proposal to join the Birkenhead Joint Line at Daresbury was successfully opposed by the LNWR. With amicable relations restored, the two railways then saw off the Nantwich-Northwich section of the Great Western Railway's attempt to reach the saltfield with its Wellington and Cheshire Junction Railway of 1860.

The Saltfield developed rapidly in the mid Nineteenth century with a vibrant export trade via Merseyside, and nationwide demand for salt both domestically and industrially. Open plan production demanded large quantities of coal and not surprisingly there was a need to break the stranglehold on transport enjoyed by the Weaver Navigation, reflected in the strong local support for the Cheshire Midland Railway of 1860 from Altrincham to Northwich which ultimately became part of the Cheshire Lines Committee, one of the country's most distinctive Joint Railways.

The Manchester South Junction and Altrincham Railway, a Joint Line promoted by the LNWR and Manchester, Sheffield and Lincolnshire Railway, had opened in 1849. The MS&LR agreed to support the Cheshire Midland extension to Northwich, but the LNWR curiously declined to do so. In 1865, Sir Edward Watkin the MS&LR's entrepreneurial Chairman, abetted by the Great Northern Railway, seized the opportunity to strike deep into LNWR and GWR territory in Cheshire and ultimately North Wales, by supporting the West Cheshire Railway of 1861 from Northwich to Helsby.

In 1862, the MS&LR and GNR had set up the Cheshire Lines Committee to manage the West Cheshire, Cheshire Midland, Stockport, Timperley and Altrincham, and Stockport and Woodley Junction railways, which saw the establishment by 1866 of an increasingly important route through South Manchester. By 1867, the CLC was a Joint Railway owned by the MS&LR, GNR and Midland railways, and by the LNER and LMS after the Grouping, remaining essentially independent until Nationalisation in 1948 when it passed to the London Midland Region of BR.

Apart from the Sentinel Railcars, its motive power came from the MS&LR and its successors the Great Central and LNER, and taken with its own distinctive traditions in buildings, rolling stock and signalling, provided a notable contrast with the LNWR/LMS tradition which mostly prevailed elsewhere in Cheshire. The CLC and its associates linked Mid Cheshire with the East Coast ports, the North Midlands coalfields, and westwards to the Mersey and GWR, providing the basis for heavy freight traffic in both directions for well over a hundred years.

The Cheshire Midland opened for passengers to Knutsford on 12th May 1862, being extended to a terminus to the west of the present Northwich station on 1st January 1863, goods services following four months later. The present station opened in May 1868 to serve trains off the Middlewich branch, being rebuilt in its current form in 1897. In the 1860s, the Northwich district bustled with the activities of over twenty salt works and numerous rock salt mines, hence the opening of the 'Northwich Salt Branches' on 17th December 1867. "Branch No 1" diverged westwards at Northwich East Junction to serve mines at Marston. "Branch No 2" curved north eastwards at Wincham across the Trent and Mersey Canal to serve various works, whilst "Branch No.3" began in the station goods yard, crossed Manchester Road and followed the line of the main street to Barons Quay, serving a variety of salt and other works and also taking coal imports from the River Weaver.

Clearly the LNWR could not remain isolated from the saltfield, and in 1863 promoted a branch from Sandbach to Northwich via Middlewich. The eight and three-quarter mile line opened for goods on 11th November 1867. The LNWR gained running powers over the West Cheshire line, and planned a triangular junction at Northwich. Passenger services were delayed until 1st July 1868 whilst the LNWR unsuccessfully tried to persuade the CLC to relocate their station westwards into the triangle area. Improved passenger accommodation and signalling were also needed at Northwich. Ironically, the south to west chord of the triangle was not completed until 16th June 1957 after some ninety years of enforced reversals for both passenger and freight services!

Winsford and Over, c. 1910: A train of ancient CLC six wheel carriages is headed by Sacre 2-4-0 No. **169** dating from 1888. The engine was placed on the duplicate list as No. **169B** in 1911 and survived as the last of the class until June 1923, although no longer at Northwich. The 2-4-0s gave way to 'F1' 2-4-2 tanks and 'J9'/'10' 0-6-0s before the arrival of the Sentinel railcar in July 1929 when Winsford shed closed. The station opened on 1st July 1870 and passenger services had a chequered history before being withdrawn for the third and final time on 1st January 1931. Note the unusual CLC shunting signal next to the locomotive.

G J C Griffiths/Winsford Historical Society

Northwich, c. 1913: An immaculate Parker Class '3' (LNER 'F1') 2-4-2 tank No. **578** of 1889 stands in the outside carriage siding, probably with stock for a Winsford service in the years immediately before the First World War. Northwich had several batches of these engines at various times between 1900 and 1942, and they performed well on the main line passenger workings.
E M Johnson Collection

The West Cheshire Railway followed a non too easy route across the Cheshire Ridge to Helsby, West Cheshire Junction, where the Birkenhead Joint Company's line to Hooton gave access to Birkenhead docks and to the GWR via Saltney. Constructional problems, principally on the 800 yard Weaver Viaduct at Northwich delayed opening until 1st September 1869 for goods, passenger services to Helsby following on 22nd June 1870. The goods extension to West Cheshire Junction opened on 14th June 1871. The Weaver Trustees demanded a clearance of sixty-one feet above the river and this was the cause of the impressive Northwich viaduct and a station three quarters of a mile from the town centre; they also prevented the extension of 'Salt Branch No. 3' across the river to Winnington, which had to be reached by the branch from Hartford, descending at I in 53, the steepest gradient on the CLC system.

This line opened on 1st September 1869 via a westward facing connection, to serve saltworks by the river, but its importance increased immeasurably with the opening of Brunner, Mond and Company's chemical enterprise at Winnington in 1873. Further west, the LNWR spur between Hartford CLC and LNW Junctions opened in March 1870, giving northbound access to the West Coast Main Line and the South Lancashire industrial districts. A complementary development was the opening in 1869 of the direct line from Weaver Junction to Runcorn and Liverpool. Until this date there had been significant interchange of passengers (via road) and goods (via canal) for Runcorn at Preston Brook.

Although goods traffic remained important on the Helsby line, the irresistible magnet was the county town of Chester, hence the promotion with CLC support, of the Chester and West

Cheshire Junction Railway in July 1865 to link Mouldsworth with the Birkenhead Joint Line at Mickle Trafford. Access to Chester General station was denied however, and the CLC was forced to build its own line to Chester Northgate, where opposition from the Cathedral authorities prevented a terminus within the city walls, and the south facing connection at Mickle Trafford remained unused until finally removed in 1903.

The LNWR and GWR were to regret their intransigence at Chester; goods services began to Northgate on 2nd November 1874, followed by passengers from 1st May 1875. Passenger services on the Helsby line ceased immediately, but seventeen years later the opening of the line from Northgate to the Wrexham, Mold and Connah's Quay railway provided the MS&LR with its springboard into North Wales and a valuable alternative route to Birkenhead docks.

In the east, several unsuccessful schemes focused on the area between Macclesfield and Knutsford. In the mid 1860s, there was local support for a line from Macclesfield via Knutsford to Warrington. The LNWR bought off the MS&LR's interest in this scheme, and a similar proposal did not survive the mini depression of 1866-67. A further Macclesfield-Knutsford scheme was still-born in 1871/2. In the early 1890s, the Lancashire, Derbyshire and East Coast Railway proposed an extension from Chesterfield to Warrington via Macclesfield with a spur to the CLC at Knutsford, no doubt with a view to the Northwich coal and chemical traffic, with the former already running at one and a half million tons per annum. However, the route through the Peak District would have been prohibitively expensive and this scheme was never a realistic possibility.

5

CONTRETEMPS AT WINSFORD
"The most important salt town in the world"

The concentration of salt works at Winsford saw the river Weaver carrying no less than 901,000 tons of salt in 1870, a prize which both the CLC and LNWR were anxious to share, despite the fact that rail transport was almost twice as expensive.

Originally, the CLC planned a freight only branch from Cuddington to Meadow Bank, but in 1868 belated plans were deposited for a southward extension from Falks Junction along the river bank to Winsford, and a northward extension to Falks Works, goods traffic commencing on 1st June 1870. A further siding to Verdin's Knightsgrange works opened in October 1876, and about six works were served between Falks Junction and Winsford. Passenger services began on 22nd June, 1870 and were soon withdrawn from 31st December 1873, but not before Sir Edward Watkin had proposed a 'Sandbach and Winsford Junction Railway' in 1872 to give access to the Potteries. Not even Watkin could facilitate this profligate scheme, but it is fascinating to imagine the line climbing past the Weaver 'flashes', crossing the West Coast Route and duplicating the Middlewich branch only some three miles to the east.

The LNWR branch to Over and Wharton developed from the mineral line opened by 1870 to Lycett's Coal Wharf and extended in 1880 to Liverpool Salt Works in Wharton. Despite the CLC's difficulties with passenger services, the LNWR clearly felt the need to serve Winsford more directly, and the station close to the town centre but approached by the steep Wharton hill, opened for passengers on 1st June 1882.

Possibly spurred by the LNWR presence, the CLC had the temerity to reintroduce passenger services from 30th April 1886, by which time many sidings had been provided but without the full signalling needed for a passenger route. Inevitably perhaps, on 25th August 1888, locomotive No. 130 on the 1215 to Cuddington was inadvertently diverted into Deakin's Over Works siding, colliding with some wagons, fortunately without serious consequences. Passenger services were again suspended from 30th November whilst the CLC pondered the cost of new signalling against an unlikely increase in traffic (there were only three 'mixed' trains each way at the time of withdrawal). Services were reinstated for the second time in seventeen years on 31st January 1892 when the Winsford Local Board obtained a ruling from the Railway Commissioners that the line's Act of Parliament obliged the CLC to provide a passenger service, a provision which secured matters for a further thirty-eight years

........*into Cheshire and the Vale Royal*

Hale, c. 1946. The well known double arched bridge, with the Hale distant signal just beyond, formed an appropriate boundary between suburbia and countryside. An LNER C13 4-4-2 tank heads for Chester in this early post-war study.   *J Peden*

The Route Described

Knutsford West c. 1912: In the zenith of Britain's railways immediately before the First World War, an immaculate GCR '9K' 4-4-2 tank (LNER C13) No. **115** takes a ten coach rake of CLC six wheeled stock away from Knutsford towards Chester. Introduced in 1903, these fine locomotives were much appreciated by enginemen and were still at work in 1957, No. **115** as BR No. **67438** being withdrawn in August of that year. The signalbox here opened in 1889 when the goods yard was relocated west of the station. The large goods shed which closed in 1965 can be seen in the distance, it was last used in 1967 to store withdrawn '8Fs' from Northwich prior to scrapping.
Real Photogaphs - R. W. Miller Collection

THROUGH KNUTSFORD AND NORTHWICH TO CHESTER

Leaving Hale, the line falls sharply at 1 in 139, crosses the River Dean and climbs at 1 in 203 to Ashley. A steady rise at 1 in 382/539/302/146 follows through verdant Cheshire countryside past Mobberley, whence a fall at 1 in 891 leads to a rise at 1 in 120 to Shaw Heath where there were once wartime petrol sidings and a siding to Knutsford Waterworks.

A sharp right hand curve with a 40mph restriction heralds Knutsford, with the line briefly in suburbia once more before climbing at 1 in 154 past the former goods yard and West Box. A long descent at 1 in 107/117 above the surrounding countryside and across the M6 leads to Plumley, whence a rise at 1 in 366 through Plumley West leads past the closed sites of the Ammonia Soda Company on the right and the Associated Octel Company on the left, before a descent at 1 in 275 past Lostock Gralam.

The line then crosses the Trent and Mersey Canal, falling at 1 in 100 past Lostock Works to Northwich East Junction where the once extensive yards fanned out on both sides and Salt Branch No.1 diverged westwards to Marston. 765 yards west was Central Cabin, controlling connections to the goods yard and locomotive depot. A further 462 yards through the not unimposing Northwich station led to Sandbach Junction, whilst the Barons Quay branch diverged from the station goods yard on the right, the original Cheshire Midland Railway terminus.

West of the station, the terraced houses surrounding the triangular junction with the Middlewich branch frequently re-echoed with the exhausts of hard worked locomotives taking a run at the mile long 1 in 100 rise across the Weaver Viaduct to Hartford East which offered panoramic views across the town and surrounding countryside. Here, the Winnington branch diverges at 1 in 76/97 offering a real challenge to heavy trains, especially the 'Hoppers'. The main line continues climbing at 1 in 300 across the base of the Hartford Triangle, within which there were once extensive sidings controlled by Hartford Exchange and Hartford North boxes. The box at Hartford and Greenbank formerly controlled the western exit from Winnington, but the power box opened here in 1979 now controls all signalling in the Northwich area.

From Hartford North, the Winnington branch falls at 1 in 116 through Oakleigh Sidings, and under the Warrington road bridge marking the limit of BR working. A brief rise at 1 in 192 past Gravel Pit Sidings leads to the site of Beswicks Road Box (closed 1953) which marks the final descent at 1 in 53 to the river Weaver, close to the Winnington Works complex.

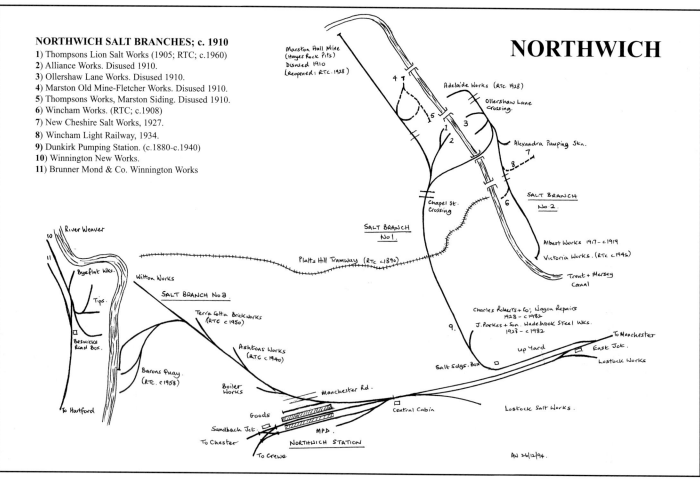

NORTHWICH

NORTHWICH SALT BRANCHES; c. 1910

1) Thompsons Lion Salt Works (1905; RTC; c.1960)
2) Alliance Works. Disused 1910.
3) Ollershaw Lane Works. Disused 1910.
4) Marston Old Mine-Fletcher Works. Disused 1910.
5) Thompsons Works, Marston Siding. Disused 1910.
6) Wincham Works. (RTC; c.1908)
7) New Cheshire Salt Works, 1927.
8) Wincham Light Railway, 1934.
9) Dunkirk Pumping Station. (c.1880-c.1940)
10) Winnington New Works
11) Brunner Mond & Co. Winnington Works

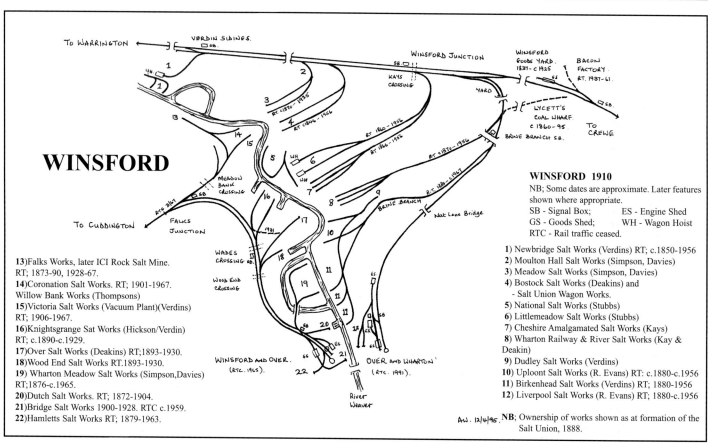

WINSFORD

13) Falks Works, later ICI Rock Salt Mine. RT; 1873-90, 1928-67.
14) Coronation Salt Works. RT; 1901-1967. Willow Bank Works (Thompsons)
15) Victoria Salt Works (Vacuum Plant)(Verdins) RT; 1906-1967.
16) Knightsgrange Sat Works (Hickson/Verdin) RT; c.1890-c.1929.
17) Over Salt Works (Deakins) RT;1893-1930.
18) Wood End Salt Works RT.1893-1930.
19) Wharton Meadow Salt Works (Simpson,Davies) RT;1876-c.1965.
20) Dutch Salt Works. RT; 1872-1904.
21) Bridge Salt Works 1900-1928. RTC c.1959.
22) Hamletts Salt Works RT; 1879-1963.

WINSFORD 1910

NB; Some dates are approximate. Later features shown where appropriate.
SB - Signal Box;   ES - Engine Shed
GS - Goods Shed;   WH - Wagon Hoist
RTC - Rail traffic ceased.

1) Newbridge Salt Works (Verdins) RT; c.1850-1956
2) Moulton Hall Salt Works (Simpson, Davies)
3) Meadow Salt Works (Simpson, Davies)
4) Bostock Salt Works (Deakins) and
   - Salt Union Wagon Works.
5) National Salt Works (Stubbs)
6) Littlemeadow Salt Works (Stubbs)
7) Cheshire Amalgamated Salt Works (Kays)
8) Wharton Railway & River Salt Works (Kay & Deakin)
9) Dudley Salt Works (Verdins)
10) Uploont Salt Works (R. Evans) RT: c.1880-c.1956
11) Birkenhead Salt Works (Verdins) RT; 1880-1956
12) Liverpool Salt Works (R. Evans) RT; 1880-c.1956

AW. 12/4/95. **NB**; Ownership of works shown as at formation of the Salt Union, 1888.

Approaching **Ashley, 2nd August 1957:** Worthy successors to the Northwich 'Directors' were the highly popular Fowler class '4' tanks, which held the fort very capably until dieselisation in 1959. No. **42365** gallops away from suburbia and into the gently undulating Cheshire countryside with the 1628 Manchester Central - Chester Northgate semi-fast, always a source of good running by Northwich crews.   *A W Martin*

The main line climbs away through a long, deep cutting at 1 in 192/120 to Hartford CLC Junction, where the LNWR spur diverges northwards to the West Coast Main Line which is crossed soon afterwards, with the CLC on a long embankment climbing at 1 in 120 towards Cuddington, a pleasant wayside station in a wide cutting. A sharp fall at 1 in 125 leads through increasingly wooded country to the former Winsford Junction, whence a climb at 1 in 116 leads through the forest to the crossing of the Cheshire Ridge at Delamere, once a delightful station but now a forest visitor's centre. The line then drops at 1 in 90 through the heart of the forest to Mouldsworth, formerly the junction for the West Cheshire branch.

Open country follows as the line falls at 1 in 95/100 past the long closed, but still extant, buildings at Barrow for Tarvin, crossing the River Gowy before climbing at 1 in 75 through Plemstall Crossing to Mickle Trafford with the Birkenhead Joint Line from Warrington to Chester coming close alongside. The junctions between the two routes enjoyed a chequered history: the first south facing connection was never used once the CLC was denied access to Chester General and ongoing disputes saw it lifted in 1903. During the Second World War, in October 1942, a north facing connection was put in to provide an alternative route to Birkenhead docks via the Chester and

Dee Marsh triangles. Only occasional light engines and empty DMU's used this connection after the war. With the closure of Chester Northgate on 7th September 1969, the line to Mouldsworth was singled and tokenless block working introduced. A new signal box was provided at Mickle Trafford, and the junctions re-laid in single track form to give north and south facing connections and a through Dee Marsh - Mouldsworth route. The latter was put out of use from 20th May 1984 following the end of steel making at Shotton, and the north facing connection was closed at the same time when steel traffic from Ravenscraig to Shotton was diverted via Wrexham. This proved unsatisfactory and the north facing junction re-opened from 31st August 1986 until the Ravenscraig traffic ceased in June 1992, the line to Dee Marsh being taken out of use from 19th October due to the condition of the track.

From Mickle Trafford, the CLC climbed steeply westwards at 1 in 73 across the Birkenhead Joint before levelling out and falling at 1 in 98 through the Chester suburbs and across the Birkenhead - Chester line to Chester East Junction where the line to Dee Marsh branched westwards with a triangular junction. To the left the extensive CLC goods yard and locomotive depot were to be seen as the line curved sharply southwards rising at 1 in 200 from South Junction to the small but well appointed Northgate terminus, just outside the city walls but significantly closer to the city centre than the rival Chester General.

TRAFFIC AT NORTHWICH

The completion of Mid Cheshire's railway system coincided with the peaking of salt production about 1880, but the subsequent decline was more than compensated by the growth of chemicals. From 1873, Brunner Mond's Winnington Works was using 600 tons of limestone per month from the Buxton quarries, bringing Midland locomotives to Northwich. By 1938 this traffic was running at 2800 tons per day, rising to 4500 tons daily by the 'Sixties. Coal came from the North Midlands, North Staffordshire and Lancashire, whilst distribution to a vast chemicals market meant that Northwich was set to become a railway centre of significant importance. In the 'Nineties, the Davis Chlorine and Bowman Thompson plants opened at Lostock, followed by the Ammonia Soda Company at Plumley West in 1908. Yard facilities were expanded in consequence and in 1897 the CLC opened an impressive new station at a cost of £8600 reflecting the status of the area as a principal traffic centre. However, the £300 annual fee for accommodating North Staffordshire trains proved prohibitive, and proposals for a Northwich-Stoke service were stillborn.

In 1911, forty-six Down and fifty-nine Up goods trains were booked daily through Northwich. The Great Central ran coal and empties from Worksop, Wigan and Annesley, and a goods service to Bidston. It reached its dominions in North Wales and Merseyside with through goods from Wrexham to Huskisson, Bidston to Guide Bridge and Hawarden to Ashbury's, together with workings from West Leigh and Godley to Bidston. CLC through goods ran from Helsby to Trafford Park, Huskisson, Godley, Manchester and Heaton Mersey, and from Chester to Godley, Hawarden to Philips Park, and the daily Chester - Manchester milk. Northwich generated much traffic in its own right with trains to Heaton Mersey, Winsford, Chester, Skelton Junction, Glazebrook, Manchester, Philips Park, Ardwick, coal from Wigan and cattle from Cornbrook. The Midland Railway ran four coal and limestone trains daily, from Kirkby, Gowhole, Ambergate and Peak Forest, Buxton and Millers Dale respectively. LNWR services included three transfers from Crewe, two minerals from Sandbach, a Harecastle-Northwich coal, Crewe-Northwich cattle, and a transfer from Warrington. There was one daily NSR mineral service from Grange Junction, returning as a goods to Sideway.

There were eleven CLC passenger trains each way between Chester and Manchester (two of them expresses), five Northwich-Manchester trains (eight in the opposite direction), and one Northwich-Cuddington and Cuddington-Manchester working. LNWR services were quite complex with around twelve trains each way, consisting of recently introduced Motor trains to Sandbach, Crewe and Nantwich, supplemented by trains from St Helens, Liverpool, Earlestown and Manchester Oxford Road to Sandbach or Crewe, many reversing at Northwich, the latter including a through coach to Euston.

The First World War brought heavy demand for Ammonium and Calcium Nitrate for armaments, and £17,000 was spent extending the up and down yards giving a western exit from Lostock Works and improving locomotive facilities. At Wincham, £11,000 provided new sidings at Victoria Works. A new WD factory, Albert Works, opened in 1916 and workpeoples trains ran

to a temporary platform at Victoria Works nearby. Lostock Gralam also had a 'munitions platform' on the upside only, a similar facility being installed at Plumley West. In 1918, 104,000 tons of chemicals came from Wincham, and 28,000 tons from Plumley with large increases from all the other Northwich plants. Gadbrook explosives siding on the Middlewich branch produced 60 tons of TNT daily. At Winnington the works was twenty-five times larger than in 1880, although salt traffic was about 50% down. Coal from North Staffordshire to John Summer's steelworks at Shotton involved reversing four or five heavy trains daily at Northwich, and then working them westwards over heavy gradients which were a problem for the relatively small 'J9' and 'J10' 0-6-0s used. Through traffic from Heaton Mersey to Northwich, Shotton and GCR services to Merseyside was also very heavy, two long refuge sidings being put in at Plumley West to stage this traffic.

The depression of the 'Twenties and 'Thirties was to some extent offset by new developments. The creation of Imperial Chemical Industries in 1926 and expansion at Wallerscote more than compensated for the closure of the Ammonia Soda works, Davis Chlorine plant and a continued decline in salt production. The flooding of the Marston salt mines in 1928 was soon followed by the opening of the New Cheshire Saltworks bringing some 9,000 tons of outward traffic and 7200 tons of coal inward. Access was via the Wincham Light Railway of some 120 yards along Chapel Street, opened in 1934. Across the road were the redundant sidings of Albert Works, recovered in the scrap drive of the Second World War. "A severe depression in the town" was recorded in the CLC minutes of 1932, whilst perishable traffic from a wide agricultural area was being lost to the roads. The Winsford passenger service was withdrawn in 1931, as was the LMS through coach to Euston. Consideration was given to extending the MSJ & A electrification to Knutsford which issued more first class season tickets than any other CLC station, but the town was still relatively small and the proposals were dropped in 1935.

Despite these problems the railway remained quite busy and in 1937 Northwich saw sixty-four passenger and one hundred and forty-three freight trains daily. On the down road there were through LNER workings from Godley to Chester, Bidston (two, one an express through goods), Dee Marsh, Wrexham and three trains to Birkenhead, iron ore empties from Stanton Junction to Bidston, Heaton Mersey-Wrexham, Manchester Central-Bidston and Huskisson-Dee Marsh through goods. On the Up road came five conditional paths for LNER cattle specials from Birkenhead Dock Road, and return equivalents of the afore-mentioned Down services. Many CLC freights were staged at Northwich, but Down through workings included two from Heaton Mersey to Helsby, a Warrington/Glazebrook-Helsby train, a Trafford Park-Helsby, with similar Up workings. The LMS Middlewich-Warrington caustic soda and its empties, which revered at Northwich, completed the through train picture.

Northwich generated much traffic in its own right. Down inward services included eleven LMS coal and limestone trains from Cheadle, Tunstead, Peak Forest and Millers Dale to Northwich, Hartford and Gravel Pit Sidings. Twelve months later

Ashley for Rostherne, c. 1915: A train for Manchester composed of CLC twelve and six wheeled coaches of the 1880s stands in the station headed by a graceful Sacre 4-4-0 No. **424B** of 1877 on a Trafford Park diagram. Even then the Chester line was a place of retirement for elderly express locomotives; the engine was already on the duplicate list and was withdrawn in 1919. *A G Ellis, courtesy of G B Ellis*

the limestone service was reorganised with four daily block trains of sixteen 44 ton capacity hoppers with '8F' power, providing a minimum of 2688 tons daily. The LNER ran coal from Barnsley, goods from Halewood, whilst the CLC ran three trains from Heaton Mersey, Godley and Trafford Park, two Heaton Mersey-Hartford Workings and the Skelton and Plumley trips. Up services involved eight LMS trains off the Middlewich branch - two from Basford Hall, coal from Lawton Junction, Grange Junction, Longport and Cliffe Vale, and a goods from Warrington. There were six CLC trains from Dee Marsh, six from Helsby, three from Winsford and pilot trips from Hartford and Chester, the latter going through to Plumley West. Virtually all these services were duplicated in the down direction, the principal CLC workings reflecting the importance of the railway in distributing ICI's products together with the remaining salt traffic. Hence two trains to Helsby, six to Dee Marsh, three each to Godley and Heaton Mersey and through goods services to Warrington CLC, Glazebrook, Manchester Central and Halewood.

There were twelve weekday Manchester - Chester passenger trains, three being evening 'expresses' running semifast to Northwich and then most stations to Chester, reached in about 1 hour 20 minutes. Eight Manchester-Northwich trains completed this rather lavish provision, together with two Altrincham-Northwich services. Twelve trains from Chester and six from Northwich ran in the opposite direction, only the 0925 from Chester being an 'express', the $38\frac{3}{4}$ miles being covered usually in about $1\frac{1}{2}$ hours by stopping train.

The LMS provided eleven trains between Crewe and Northwich, about half being motor trains some of which worked through to Acton Bridge or Warrington or turned round at Sandbach. Earlstown and Liverpool-Crewe services reversed at Northwich, whilst two services to Warrington and one to Ditton Junction started from Northwich. On Saturdays, there was a Sandbach-Blackpool train, but no corresponding up service.

The Second World War saw severe congestion, with traffic 26% up on the already demanding pre war figure. In addition to the usual traffics, pressure to move goods to the Merseyside ports was intense and many traffic flows had to be diverted away from the Northwich area. Hence CLC traffic from Liverpool to the GWR was sent via the LMS, traffic from Trafford Park to Helsby was no longer staged at Northwich and coal traffic was reorganised into block workings, so in 1942 Winnington was served daily by five block trains from the LNER, one from North Staffordshire and two from Yorkshire via Cheadle. In the Northwich yards there were never enough sidings to shunt for individual destinations and every Sunday witnessed a desperate battle to 'get straight' for the following week. Chronic staff shortages, made worse by a local housing shortage compounded these problems and two sleeping cars provided temporary accommodation for staff drafted in from elsewhere. Eventually, Government finance provided £13,000 for new reception roads and sidings in the down yard, lengthening of the up loops to take sixty-nine wagons whilst allowing simultaneous shunting in the up yard, and better access and watering facilities at the locomotive depot. Elsewhere, £15,000 saw the restoration of the Mickle Trafford connection and double tracking and lengthening of the Helsby branch junction at Mouldsworth. At Shaw Heath, a petrol depot was put in on the up side in 1942, to serve the numerous US

Army camps in the area, and with the approach of the Normandy invasion, Knutsford yard was equipped with tank loading ramps. Not all effects of the war were beneficial however; the LMS withdrew passenger services between Northwich and Acton Bridge on 30th June 1941.

The Post war years brought little respite with the Winnington branch at saturation point handling 1000 wagons per day over the steeply graded single line. A threefold increase was expected by 1950, forcing ambitious improvements; the construction of a new reception and departure yard at Oakleigh, half way down the Winnington branch, and a new yard at Gorstage alongside the main line at Hartford LNW Junction, linked to the Winnington complex by ICI's 1¹/₂ mile Wallerscote Light Railway. The new facilities opened in February 1953, with the yards linked by heavy trip workings to Northwich, whilst the use of Hartford Exchange sidings was much reduced. ICI's daily requirement was now 4500 tons of limestone, 3500 tons of coal, with 5000 tons of finished products, a throughput of 1500 wagons daily at both new yards which, with the needs of Lostock Works, gave the basis for a bustling railway scene lasting well into the 'seventies. An important development in June 1957 was the opening of the the South to West chord off the Middlewich branch, giving opportunities for much freight traffic to the Wirral and Dee Marsh to bypass Crewe and the for West Coast passenger diversions at weekends.

Before the War, Chester races were a source of much excursion traffic, involving the opening of an addition block post west of Mickle Trafford. Chester Cup Day, 4th May 1927 for example, produced seventeen specials powered by a variety of GC 'Atlantics', 4-6-0s, and the inevitable 'J10s' once all other resources had been exhausted! Most trains ran to Liverpool Road, going empty to Dee Marsh with the locomotives serviced at Northgate. Chester remained a popular destination for evening excursions from Manchester until the late 'Fifties, and well into the 'Sixties the evening services from Northgate were often crowded with day-trippers. Northwich saw significant excursion traffic, often using coaching sets stabled there between commuter workings. There was a substantial following of the town's two football teams, and 'J39' 0-6-0s could sometimes be seen at the 'capital' of the LMS when Northwich Victoria took on Crewe Alexandra. As late as 1965/6 Northwich '8Fs' could be seen competently heading for North Wales or the Fylde Coast, but increasing car ownership and strict use of resources have long since put an end to such traffic.

By the late 'Fifties most trains were worked by modern LMS or BR locomotives. The last GC 4-4-2 tanks disappeared in 1957 and the 'Directors' twelve months later. The 1957/8 winter service saw eleven trains each way, four Northwich-Manchester returns, a Cuddington-Manchester and early morning Chester-Altrincham and Altrincham-Northwich trains, timings being no faster than in CLC days. Between 1957 and 1960 there were also daily diversions of Manchester expresses and parcels services because of the Crewe-Manchester electrification, including a variety of Birmingham and West of England trains, and the 'Pines Express'. In the summer of 1959, the Chester service was increased to half hourly frequency and Derby 'lightweight' class 108 DMUs took over. This however left insufficient paths for the freight service and an hourly frequency was restored with the

winter timetable. Periodic shortages of DMU's saw some steam diagrams retained until 1961, and until 1966 the 0721 from Chester and 1740 from Manchester were often steam, the latter offering its driver the experience of steam, diesel and electric traction all in one shift! Regrettably this period saw the end of the 'Dodger', when services between Crewe and Northwich were withdrawn from 4th January 1960.

Northwich remained a very busy place to the end of the steam era. In 1960-61, sixty-three Up and fifty-eight Down freights were booked daily together with the trippers to Gorstage and Oakleigh which ran at least three times per shift. On the Up road there were services to Sheffield, Warrington CLC, Glazebrook (two), Ferme Park, Whitemoor and Pyewipe. Coal emptics went to Heaton Mersey, Mansfield, Warsop and Stainforth, with six sets of limestone hoppers to Great Rocks Junction. The Skelton pilot now ran to Knutsford only. Inward traffic and empties came from Saltney, Carlisle, Ellesmere Port (two), Crewe (three), Warrington LNW (two), Dee Marsh (four), Birkenhead, Bamfurlong, Bridgewater, and coal trains from Alsager, Chanters Siding, and Grange Junction (two). Twenty-three through services included general freight from Bidston and Dee Marsh to Sheffield, the two Saltney-Trafford Park vans, mineral empties from Dee Marsh to Cheadle and Wath, and from Bidston to Cadeby Colliery and Godley. From the Middlewich branch came limestone empties to Great Rocks, and much traffic for the new chord line.

The down road was not quite so busy. General freights van to Crewe (three), Dee Marsh (three), Saltney, Shotwick, Warrington LNW, Birkenhead and Bamfurlong, together with the pickups to Winsford (two) and Chester. There was a Soda ash train to Clock Face, and empties to Longport, Etruria and Chanters Siding. Terminating services were dominated by coal and limestone, but included mixed freight from Halewood CLC and the return Knutsford pick up. Coal came from Mottram (three), Mansfield, Gowhole, Ollerton and Newstead, the pride of the line being the six hopper workings from Peak Forest. Through services involved general freight from Heaton Mersey to Birkenhead and Dee Marsh, Broughton Lane and Godley to Birkenhead, Trafford Park, Warrington CLC and Glazebrook to Saltney, Derby to Shotwick, and a Northampton-Warrington fitted freight via Middlewich. Trainload services included the Middlewich-Warrington Soda ash, Tunstead-Shotwick limestone, Barnsley and Colwick to Ellesmere Port empty tanks, seven Mottram - Shotwick coal services and one from Wath.

The 'Sixties saw some changes and rationalisation. From 1962 Northwich was part of the Liverpool Division and this brought an end to some of the traditional routings such as the turns to Glazebrook and Warrington CLC and the through services to the Wrexham and Birkenhead areas. By the end of the decade also, the routing of traffic southwards over the GWR via Saltney had ceased. New traffics arising from ICI's Runcorn operations included the Tunstead-Runcorn Covhops, Runcorn-Grimsby tanks and coal between Yorkshire and Runcorn. Long distance tank workings from Stanlow to the North Midlands also added to the through traffic. The closure of Middlewich ICI works in 1962 brought an end to the caustic soda train to Warrington, and the limestone workings to Peak Forest which had transferred from the

Ashley, 26th June 1948: Before nationalisation a large variety of goods trains operated from Godley Junction to the Northwich, Wrexham and Birkenhead areas. After 1945 these Gorton turns often produced examples of the rapidly disappearing varieties of GCR 4-6-0s, which also worked some passenger turns as well. Mixed traffic 'Glenalmond' No. **1357** *Lord Roberts of Kandahar* heads a westbound freight. Built in 1914, she was the last of the class when withdrawn in April 1949. *J D Darby*

LNWR route via Stockport about 1950. Offsetting this loss of traffic expansion at the Wirral Chemical plants and John Summers steelworks saw significant increase in petrol and coal traffic from North Staffordshire and the North Midlands. New traffic flows included Soda ash block workings to Corkickle and Larbert which survived into the 'Nineties.

However, the history of the last twenty years is one of much rationalisation. Transfers via Crewe ended in 1972, and succeeding years brought an end to general freight distribution by wagonload, decimating many of the originating services to Birkenhead, Saltney and the former LMS and LNER systems in the east. By the 'Eighties there was no future for wagonload: the trip workings to the ICI yards ceased in 1982, and trains were concentrated in block loads, with the closure of the up yard, Gorstage Yard and the Wallerscote Light Railway which was lifted in 1989. When Northwich train crew depot closed in 1984, booked trains were down to thirty-nine up and thirty-three down services, all trainload, air or vacuum braked services, not all running every day.

The last ten years have seen further contraction, culminating in the end of regular freight services west of Hartford CLC Junction. The end of steelmaking at Shotton in the early 'Eighties brought an end to much valuable coal traffic, and the closure of the West Cheshire branch from September 1991 completed the process. Perhaps we will live to regret the wholesale transfer of so much freight traffic to the roads: at Northwich the station goods yard is now occupied by a supermarket and the locomotive depot was finally demolished in 1991. Happily the 'Hoppers', impressively double headed by class 37s and running in fewer but even larger train loads survived until 1997, but it is generally a desolate railway scene compared to the activity of former years. Air braked Hoppers were temporarily hired in from 1998, and new JHA hoppers are now in order. Since 1992 passenger services have been diverted from Altrincham via Stockport to Manchester, but now run to an interesting variety of destinations on the Lancashire coast. The basic hourly frequency remains, but it still takes $1^1/_2$ hours to get from Manchester to Chester via the CLC!

Ashley

Ashley, 6th August 1962: There is no M56 to disturb the rural tranquillity in this view. The characteristic Cheshire Midland buildings - slightly more ornate here in view of the proximity of Tatton Park - are seen to good effect, together with the railwaymen's cottages before the signal box which was opened in 1886 and abolished on 14th June 1964. The goods yard closed on 6th March 1961, and from 1871 to 1939 there was also a siding on the up side for a private coal wharf on Lord Egerton's Tabley estate. The station was destaffed from 3rd November 1975 and the buildings still await a suitable alternative use.

D Chatfield

West of Ashley, 3rd May 1947: In 1941, after an absence of eleven years, superannuated express locomotives were again allocated to Northwich to work out their last years - a pattern to be repeated until 1957. The 1941 arrivals were the Pollitt '11A' class of 1897 (LNER 'D6') and by 1947 the shed housed the last two examples Nos. **2101** and **2106**. The former is seen heading the 1631 from Manchester Central.

J D Darby

Mobberley, c. 1967: '8F' No. **48676** rolls eastwards with a train of shock hoods carrying finished steel from Dee Marsh. The standard Cheshire Midland buildings with the station house set at $90°$ to the platform and offices and buildings adjoining are evident, with the roof of the latter extended to form a covered waiting area. The signal box of 1886 is still in operation, controlling lifting barriers installed in 1978. The station closed to goods in October 1963, being destaffed in December 1976. The not unattractive buildings are now in use as business premises. *N R Knight*

(Right) **Mobberley Station, c. 1967:** A view looking in the Up direction towards Manchester. *BR - LMR*

Mobberley

Mobberley Station, c. 1965. The solidly built and carefully detailed Cheshire Midland buildings are seen in this official view. Note that in the age of the 'Beatles' and universal use of electrical appliances in the home, the station remains oil lit.

BR - LMR

Mobberley, 13th July 1966. The chimney stacks to both the booking office and waiting rooms have been modified, but otherwise the fine detail of the station buildings persists - extended eves, canopy over the entrance, the carefully arched windows and the fence protecting the station master's garden.

BR - LMR

Mobberley, 18th October 1912. A somewhat restricted view of the level crossing and station buildings, together with the Down starting signal.

J M Ryan

Mobberley, July 1959: Heaton Mersey's Stanier class '3' tank No. **40094** slips quietly away with an evening train for Chester. By no means the best of the Stanier breed, these machines were compared most unfavourably with the GCR 4-4-2 tanks and the Ivatt class '2' variety, especially on the steep gradients west of Northwich.
T Lewis, courtesy N Preedy

(Right) Mobberley, 10th June 1965. A study of the Up platform waiting shelter and booking ofice. These were typical of the secondary facilities provided at most Cheshire Midland and West Cheshire stations. ***BR - LMR***

Motive power at Mobberley (1), 9th July 1949: Northwich received its first 'Director' 4-4-0s - the original 'D10s' - in the autumn of 1947. They replaced the 'D6s' and by 1949 the 'D9s' had gone, but the improved 'D11s' remained until 1958. 'D10' No. **62650** *Prince Henry* heads a down train interestingly composed of an MSJ & A suburban set, displaced by the Altrincham - Manchester electrification of 1931. *J D Darby*

Motive power at Mobberley (2), 9th July 1949: Another example of the interesting variety of locomotives used on the Chester line at the end of the war was the highly effective GCR 'J11' 'Pom Pom' 0-6-0 of which Northwich had two, Nos. 4367 and **4453** in 1947 - 53. The latter is caught making a smart departure with a down service from Mobberley. *J D Darby*

Motive power at Mobberley (3), 9th July 1949: At times of pressure, 'N5' 0-6-2 tanks appeared on mainline freight work as well as passenger turns. They were not too well suited to heavy goods work and inadequate brake power could easily result in runaways with unwary crews. No. **69293** is seen coping with quite a substantial westbound through freight.
J D Darby

Motive power at Mobberley (4) 9th July 1949: Towards the end of the war, 2-8-0 freight locomotives at last became available to displace the 'J10' 0-6-0s on some freight work, and especially so after the Woodhead electrification in 1954. Thompson '01' No. **3901** heads westwards through Mobberley. GC '04s', and 'WD' 2-8-0s (and the 'USA' variety during the war) were also seen, whilst on the LMS side, Stanier '8Fs' were increasingly common.
J D Darby

Shaw Heath, 2nd July 1950: For years before nationalisation, the Pollitt '9D' 0-6-0s (LNER 'J10') were the CLC's 'go anywhere, do anything' loco-motive. The whole range of duties - passenger and freight - was tackled, no mean tribute to a small, unsuperheated locomotive of Victorian vintage, although they had to be fired 'just right', otherwise a stop form 'blow up' was inevitable. No. **65161** is being worked hard - with evidence of a burnt smokebox door - on a down passenger in early BR days.

J D Darby

Shaw Heath, 11th February 1967: Stanier '8F' No. **48324** powers away from the Knutsford slack with mineral empties returning to the Yorkshire pits in an evocative study which aptly recalls the grand work the '8Fs' did in the last years of steam. The safety valves are sizzling supporting the urgent staccato followed by the drill beat of hurrying wagon wheels, a sound absent from BR for nearly thirty years now! Nearby on the Down side was a coal yard serving the steam engines of Knutsford Water Works, and a World Ward Two petrol depot opened on the up side in 1943, but the signal box here had closed by 1955.

A W Martin

Nearing **Knutsford, 28th October 1967.** The peace of the countryside is rudely shattered as a Stanier 8F No. **48253** (8C-Speke Junction) battles noisily westwards with the heavy lunchtime 8F56 Tunstead - Runcorn 'covhops', heading for the ICI plants at Weston Point. The last remnants of the bridge to the right of the engine were removed in 1984.

(Below) The line through **Knutsford** station was built on the level, reached after negotiating a short sharp adverse gradient of 1 in 120 through the Shaw Heath district of the town. The train is approaching the confines of the station, the signal box (Knutsford East) is to the right of the locomotive exhaust.

Both: E F Bentley

Knutsford, 6th June 1962. Leaving with what is the evening Crewe - Manchester Mayfield parcels train is LNER built K3 Class 2-6-0 No. **61853**. The locomotive had worked to Northwich ealier in the day double heading a passenger train. It is also thought that this was the last time a member of this class appeared on the Chester line. Beyond the pilasters of King Street bridge, the line up of wagons indicates a still healthy coal traffic, which was to remain in being until 1969.

D Chatfield

Knutsford, 1937. Football 'specials' have provided the railways with a great deal of traffic over the years. The sight of this unidentified LNER 'J10', with the words 'Play Up County' on its smokebox door, provokes memories of one of the more succesful periods enjoyed by Stockport County Football Club, it's promotion year of 1937. A spring visit to Chester justified this second train with large numbers of supporters that would swell the 'gate' to beyond the 15000 mark. Note the Knutsford 'running-in' board of cast metal serif lettering on a wooden background, the regular alternative being a cast concrete version. Until the early 'Sixties, such excursion trains were a regular feature of operations - Blackpool, Rhyl and New Brighton being popular destinations, whilst evening excursions to Chester were not unknown.

E R Morten

(Right) **Knutsford, c. 1968:** Driver 'Spud' Woodier brings two Derby lightweight class 108 DMU's bound for Manchester into the station. Introduced in 1959, they had taken over most services by 1961 and were still at work thirty years later. The Down platform awning with its ridge and furrow carriage landing dated from 1889, but had sadly disappeared by 1977. The Down side buildings have since been sold off and facilities concentrated on the modernised Up side buildings after the coal yard ceased operating about 1969.

British Railways,
courtesy D R McIntosh

the 'New' and the 'Old'

(Centre) **Knutsford, 1937.** Over thirty years separate the views of trains alongside Knutsford's Up platform. Both types would give many years of sterling service, although the longevity of the Gorton built locomotives of the Great Central Railway, represented here in LNER days by No. **5454** would outstrip their modern counterparts. Already thirty two years old when this photograph was taken, this Class C13 tank would be renumbered **7431** in 1946 before being allocated No **67431** by British Railways, an identity it carried until withdrawal in 1956.

(Left) **A close up of Adams Hill** entrance to the station in October 1973. Such lavish facilities were subsequently rationalised when the buildings on this side of the station were closed and converted to business premises several years later. ***BR-LMR***

Knutsford

Incuded on this page are three views of the buildings which overlooked Adams Hill.

(Right and Below) **Downside buildings exterior 1973.** The lavish facilities provided by the Cheshire Midland are much in evidence.

(Inset-centre) **Downside booking office exterior entrance, c. 1973.** The distinguished surroundings should be noted, together with the advertisement for the now much lamented 'Inter City' organisation, one of the most successful marketing slogans ever, although never directly a facility of the CLC!　　　　　***BR - LMR***

(Above) **Knutsford, 17th June 1967.** Stanier '8F' No **48735,** a Northwich based engine since March 1965, stands in the Up platform with the 0456 Crewe to Mayfield (Manchester) parcels train. *A W Martin*

(Left-centre) **Knutsford, June 1954.** The 'Directors', or Class D11 4-4-0s, provided the motive power for passenger trains on the Chester line for many years. Here we see Northwich based engine No. **62664** *Princess Mary* alongside the Up platform with a train bound for Manchester Central. *G W Sharpe*

(Left) The Up platform canopy was a spacious affair. This early 1970's view illustrates how few changes had been made over the years - note the decorative matchboard effect to the rear of the shelter. The small timber built 'Booking Office' had for many years been located outside the shelter facing passengers approaching from the Toft Road entrance. Interesting to note that the small canopy has been retained despite being positioned under another roof ! *BR-LMR*

(Above) **Knutsford, c. 1973.** The other of the entrances to Knutsford station was at the junction of Toft Road and Adams Hill. This unpretentious 'gateway', giving access to and from both platforms, was arguably more convenient than the 'Town Centre' approach via King Street. *(Centre)* A view west along the Down platform beneath the canopy of the main station buildings and taken looking in the direction of Northwich and Chester. The myriad of British Railways corporate signs shows the extent of the facilities provided at this busy station. *(Below)* Another view west at platform level but this time nearer to the Toft Road entrance. Through the bridge opening it is possible to see the site of the former goods yard once controlled by Knutsford West signal box. The shunting signal to the right allowed movement to the siding that can be seen in the distance. ***BR-LMR***

Plumley Bank, 20th July 1960: Robinson '04' 2-8-0 No. **63719** climbs above the surrounding countryside up to Knutsford with iron ore tipplers probably returning as coke empties from Dee Marsh to Yorkshire. The GC 'Tinies' were a grand freight locomotive, and many served abroad in both World Wars. They were a familiar sight until displaced by LMS power by about 1962. Northwich men had a healthy respect for them, but came to prefer the all round versatility of the Stanier '8F' which was just as strong, but with a much better turn of speed. *D Chatfield*

Plumley, c. 1955: The well stocked bicycle shed points to another age as 'D11' 'Director' No. **62664** *Princess Mary* hurries the 1628 Manchester - Chester semi-fast through the station. Northwich men really moved with this train and its slipstream, regularly wrought havoc to the neatly arranged station surroundings, much to the chagrin of Stationmaster Cassleton! The engine and men took over the 1308 from Northwich, going ECS to Cornbrook before setting off for Chester at 1628, and there were numerous attempts to get most of the way to Chester on one firing! Returning on the 1925 from Chester, the engine continued to Manchester whilst the crew finished the rest of their shift on disposal duties. *D Cooper*

Plumley, c. 1965. The signal box has just closed, but the buildings are still in good order. The rural situation of the station is much in evidence, but there was useful commuter traffic to Manchester. ***BR - LMR***

A Royal Occasion

Plumley, November 1957: The Middlewich pilot No. **44155** was promoted to head the Royal Train into the siding when it spent the night of 21/22 November in Plumley yard en route from Euston to the Metropolitan Vickers factory at Baguley. The Duke of Edinburgh was on the train and the pilot crew, led by Driver Jimmy Jones, were under strict orders to keep the engine quiet! The train engine is class '5' No. **45032** which had worked from Crewe. Plumley closed to goods on 3rd February 1963, but the yard has since been put to good use as an animal sanctuary. ***D Cooper***

Plumley

Plumley, c.1958: Class '5' No. **45044** brings a diverted Sunday Manchester - Birmingham express through the station which was immaculately kept at this time with prize winning gardens, and was known as Plumbley until 1st May 1945. The traditional railwaymen's cottages are just out of the picture on the Up side, set at 90° to the platform. The oil lit station lamps should be noted, whilst Plumley bank stretches away in the distance. The signalbox closed in January 1965, with the station partially destaffed some ten years later.

T Lewis, courtesy N E Preedy

Plumley, 27th April 1965. A close up of the Down platform buildings. Notice from the posters that the famous 'Double Arrow' railway symbol has recently made an appearance and that we are now into the era of corporate publicity! The buildings have latterly been tastefully converted into business premises, appropriately approached by distant and home signals.

BR-LMR

(Right) **Booking Office interior, 27th April 1965.** The fitted drawers, ticket racks and date stamping machine, together with the traditional double facing window mounted railway clock, are all features which have undergone marked change in recent years, if indeed they exist at all with most CLC stations being de-staffed. The pointed window arch, with ornate framing sometimes described as four centred, of this and all Cheshire Midland buildings should be noted.

BR-LMR

Plumley

(Left) **Plumley, a snapshot of the 'Fifties:** Northwich Passenger Guard Arthur Woodier conveys an air of competent authority and pride in the job, as do the Chester crew in charge of Ivatt class '2' tank No. **41234**. Driver Ted Watkins began his career on the LNWR at Tredegar, moving to Chester LMS depot in 1939 and to Chester Northgate on promotion to Driver in 1951. Fireman Maurice Vaughan spent ten years at Northgate, but left when steam finished in 1959. The Ivatt tanks arrived at Northgate in 1953, replacing the 'C13' and 'N5' tanks, together with the ineffective '2P' 4-4-0s which were sometimes borrowed from Chester LMS depot. The photograph dates from about 1954. *D Cooper*

(Right) **The Upside waiting shelter-cum-Booking Office, 27th April 1965.** The interior is characteristic of most of the secondary shelters between Altrincham and Chester. Note the small booking office facility, oil lamp, lack of heating and details of services to Manchester Central.

BR-LMR

Plumley West

Plumley West, 7th May 1966: District Relief Signalman Albert Booth watches Fairburn class '4' tank No. **42081** passing with empty stock going to Northwich after working a Manchester - Knutsford May Day special. The signalbox and sidings opened in February 1908 for the Ammonia Soda Company's works on the up side, a rather unsuccessful enterprise taken over by Brunner Mond in 1916 and closed in 1919. The long refuge sidings with their distinctive CLC signals were installed during World War I to relieve congestion at Northwich, being used until the late 'Fifties for crew changes between up and down Dee Marsh - Wath trains. They remained until the late 'Eighties when a derailment saw plain track installed. To the right of the guards van was the site of the 1916 munitions platform on the up side, whilst the photographer is standing near the site of a board crossing and ticket office. The oil barrel in the foreground was essential for signal and signal box lights at the time of the photograph. *A Wilkinson*

Plumley West, 26th August 1966: Ivatt class '2' No. **46440** heads the Knutsford pick up. Behind the engine are two tanks for the Associated Octel plant, in the background, which will be put off on the return journey, the remainder of the train being domestic coal for Knutsford. On the right is the site of the Ammonia Soda Company's works, whilst on the left were sidings for Brunner Mond's brine pumping station dating from about 1923, later used by Messrs. S Hutton & Co., railway contractors. The siding for the Octel plant dated from November 1938, but closed in 1989. Raw materials included lead ingots from Australia, sea water from Hayle and coal for the boilers. In the foreground was the site of the 400 foot long down munitions platform opened in 1916, which closed soon after the end of the war. *A Wilkinson*

Plumley West, 26th August 1966: The typical CLC lever frame and block instruments are seen to good effect, and in 1966 the box was still lit by a single oil light. Note the Cheshire Lines builders plate to the rear of the frame. The box still survives in 2000, along with Knutsford East and Mobberley. *A Wilkinson*

(Right) **Lostock Gralam, 26th June 1958:** A Fowler tank, unusually employed on the Knutsford pick up, shunts the yard. The railwaymen's cottages have only a short future, being demolished by 1963. ICI's Lostock Works is seen in the background, being established in 1891 by Bowman Thompson & Co. Until the 'Fifties there was considerable milk traffic, and in 1926 a special ramp was constructed from the station bridge to the up platform to facilitate the handling of milk churns. With the station destaffed, the not unattractive buildings are currently very neglected. **D Chatfield**

(Below) **Lostock Gralam, 13th July 1966.** The station had fairly recently passed into the hands of the Liverpool Divisional Manager and is looking quite smart having received a new coat of paint, whilst the signage of the 'fifties era still survives. Today's building looks positively desolate by comparison but may eventually be usefully developed. **(BR-LMR)**

Lostock Gralam, c. 1955. Driver Don France brings Heaton Mersey '4F' No. **44379** and a Down freight past the signal box installed in 1886. In 1891 it was moved 100 yards towards Northwich, possibly in connection with the opening of the Davis Chlorine Process plant nearby. The extensive yard at Lostock was explained by these works which closed in the 'Twenties, although the site remained rail connected through the 'Fifties when occupied by Harris Rond Services. The yard closed on 3rd August 1964, and the box had disappeared by 1969.   *D Cooper*

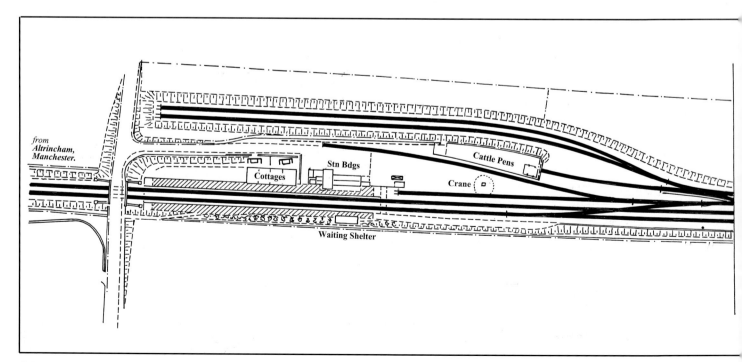

(Right) Lostock Gralam goods yard, c. 1954: Northwich Goods Guard George Drinkwater at work in Lostock Yard. George knew his job and was adept at organising shunting operations with the minimum of bother, a trait much appreciated by local engine crews. The tank wagon behind is bound for the Associated Octel plant and represented valuable traffic until the removal of lead from petrol decimated the operation in the late 'Eighties. *D Cooper*

(Left) Lostock Gralam, c. 1954: Porter Walter Dutton watches BR Standard '5 No. **73031** arrive with the 0840 Chester - Manchester. This was a Derby Compound diagram which involved a fill in trip to Chester, outward on the 0555 from Manchester. The locomotive is temporarily fitted with a Westinghouse pump for trials with air braked freight trains on the Midland Division. In the yard on the left was the site of the single munitions platform on the down side, operational during the First World War. *D Cooper*

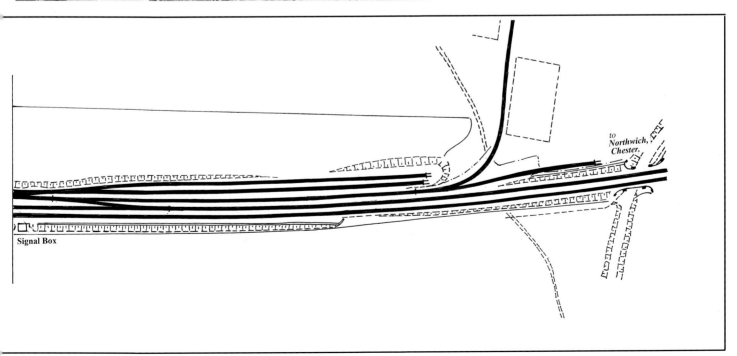

Signal Box

to Northwich, Chester.

(Left) **Lostock Booking Office, 27th April 1965.** There are more storage facilities than at Plumley, presumably reflecting the much greater freight traffic at Lostock. Electric lighting has reached the office and was shortly to be installed on the platforms. **BR-LMR**

Lostock Gralam

(Below) **Lostock Gralam, 13th July 1966.** The platform entrance at Lostock for the Ticket Office. Day return offers to local stations are evident, as are the platform scales, now a long vanished station feature! The shelter at the end of the building was not original, being added to this and other stations after about 1920.

....continued below

(Right) Northwich East Junction, 21st March 1953: 'Director' No. **62650** *Prince Henry* drifts smartly down the bank from Lostock with a Chester passenger service. The lines to the west lead to the up yard, the siding on the right being one of the access points to Lostock Works. Significant extensions to the siding facilities were necessary hereabouts to cope with the traffic during World War Two, but the up yard was closed in the early 'Eighties. *N Fields*

(Centre) Wincham Brook Bridge, Salt Branch No 1, October 1966: Ivatt 2-6-0 No. **46405** returns to Northwich with the Marston branch freight. Only residual export consignments of 'English Crown' salt from the New Cheshire

..........Saltworks via Ellesmere Port remained - hardly a lucrative business as can be seen! The line closed beyond Parkes steel siding from 15th March 1968. *A Wilkinson*

(Right) Parkes Siding, Salt Branch No 1, c. 1949. 'J10' No. **65169** shunts Wadebrook Steelworks sidings alongside the well used rails of the Marston branch. The siding opened in 1924, and nearby was the siding of Charles Roberts & Co, later Wagon Repairs Ltd, dating from 1923, which provided traffic for the final stub of the Salt Branch No 1 which closed finally about 1982. The signals in front of the Manchester Road bridge belong to Salt Sidings box, closed about 1951 and demolished by 1954. Fireman Ron Boden appears to be doing the driving. *J C Lewis*

Chapel Street Crossing, Wincham, Salt Branch No. 1 October 1966: Fireman Terry Brooker surveys the scene as No. **46405** returns empty salt hoppers to the New Cheshire Works. Only exceptionally low empty wagon rates were keeping this traffic on rail at this time. To the left, the track divided, Salt Branch No. 1 leading to Thompson's Lion Salt Works and the site of Marston Hall mine. Salt Branch No. 2 climbed steeply over the Trent and Mersey Canal to reach the New Cheshire Works - a hazardous piece of railway in wet conditions! In their hey day, these lines were busy enough to be fully signalled with gateboxes and crossing keeper's cottages here and at the Ollershaw Lane crossings, which were abolished about 1926. *A Wilkinson*

Marston Hall Mine, 1923: Originally Hayes Rock Pits, this rock salt mine was located at the end of Salt Branch No. 1 and closed in 1928 due to flooding. Two other mines - Pool mine and Marston Old - were located on the branch, but had closed by then. *Northwich*, a Falcon Engine Co. product of 1884 stands with a rake of typical Salt Union wagons containing rock salt for export, and was subsequently transferred to Stoke Works, Worcestershire. The branch remained in situ to serve wartime installations, and coal merchants on the old mine sites but closed in 1946/47. It was truncated beyond Ollershaw Lane about 1961, the remaining stub being used for wagon storage until the 'Lion' works ceased to use rail transport, shortly afterwards.

B S Jeuda Collection

Ollershaw Lane, May 1966: Ivatt 2-6-0 No. **46517** was imported from Springs Branch for the LCGB's 'Cheshire Cat' brake van tour of the Cheshire salt branches in May and August 1966, since Northwich did not have any green - or clean - Class 2s on the allocation! Almost at the end of Salt Branch No. 2, the lines to the right lead to the New Cheshire Works, with the site of Rayner's Salt Works (closed before 1910) on the left. The overhead brine pipe, a characteristic feature above or alongside many local railways, is a reminder that steam pumps were once a lucrative source of coal traffic. In the hands of Driver Harry Greenwood, the participants undoubtedly enjoyed a lively afternoon! *J M Tolson*

Ollershaw Lane, Salt Branch No. 2, October 1966: *English Crown No. 1* stands at the end of the branch, which until 1928 extended a further 500 yards across Ollershaw Lane to Adelaide Works which flooded in that year. This apparently rural scene once bustled with saltworks, and Ollershaw Lane gate box stood on stilts to protect it from flooding due to salt subsidence. The Peckett, built in 1919, arrived from the National Smelting Co., Avonmouth in 1934 and remained until the end of rail traffic. Never enjoying the luxury of a shed, it was scrapped on site in 1969.

A Wilkinson

Salt Branch No. 2, October 1966: The New Cheshire Saltworks, developed in the late 'Twenties, forms the background as its Peckett 0-4-0ST *English Crown No. 1*, the last steam industrial to work in Mid Cheshire, approaches Salt Branch No. 2 curving in from the right. Directly ahead, the branch originally continued across Chapel Street to Victoria Works, which together with Albert Works was busy with munitions in 1916 - 18 and boasted a platform for munitions workers. Salt production had ceased here by 1942, but the opening of the New Cheshire Works saw the promotion of the 'Wincham Light Railway' of 1934, which ran along Chapel Street (later within the Works boundary) to connect with the CLC. *A Wilkinson*

(Above) **Northwich, c. 1948:** The ravages of years of uncontrolled brine pumping in the form of Ashton's flash are only too evident in this aerial view. The area is bordered to the east by Salt Branch No. 1, and to the west by Salt Branch No. 3. In the top right hand corner is Chapel Street, Wincham (**1**), with Salt Branch No. 2 diverging to the right, the connection to 'Lion' Works in the centre, and Branch No. 1 continuing to Marston Hall (**2**). Northwich station with its goods yard busy with traffic is at the bottom of the picture, whilst a 'J10' heads a train from Baron's Quay across the Manchester Road (**3**) as a main line freight comes through the station. *ICI Chemicals & Polymers Ltd*

Manchester Road Crossing, 5th November 1908: Mrs Le Neve Foster of Wilmslow made an unfortunate choice of transport for a visit to Chester when her chauffeur driven car failed to obey the Flagman and collided with the Barons Quay trip with fatal results. A sombre crowd examines the remains of the vehicle which was demolished by the brake van as the train was propelled from Northwich Goods Yard. The siding to the 'Boiler Works' is in the background, with the main branch continuing right towards Barons Quay.

T Booth Collection

Northwich, 21st February 1946: This aerial panorama shows ICI's Lostock Works (**1**) and the western extremity of Lostock Gralam yard in the bottom left hand corner, where Harris Road Services Depot, formerly the site of Davis Chlorine plant, is still rail connected (**2**). Bottom right are the abandoned sites of Victoria and Albert Works (**3**), with the New Cheshire Saltworks to the west, just off the photograph, served by the Wincham Light Railway at the eastern extremity of Salt Branch No. 2. In the centre is Northwich East Junction (**4**) with the Marston branch diverging westwards south of the up yard, serving the sidings of W Parkes & Sons and Charles Roberts & Co., together with the abandoned spur to Dunkirk Pumping Station (**5**). The old gable roof of the MPD (**6**) can be seen west of the estate of brand new prefabs, which still survive, whilst Salt Branch No. 3 goes westwards from the station goods yard, across the Manchester Road to Barons Quay (**7**). The Middlewich branch curves away at Sandbach Junction, top left. *R C H M*

Central Northwich, 1955: In the mid 'Fifties, the 1340SO Manchester - Chester was booked to be double headed to Northwich. Chester shed often used Ivatt 2-6-2 tanks, and the Northwich engine returning to shed was usually a 'Director', but all manner of combinations were possible, including pairs of '2P' 4-4-0s. Here No. **62664** *Princess Mary* and Ivatt tank No. **41215** approach Central Cabin. The post carrying the Northwich East distant and Central's up starter is about to be replaced by a BR structure. Note the Midland Railway Pullman Car in the yard doing duty as an office - it had disappeared by 1957. Also, long since gone, are the Fog signalman's hut on the left, and the water tower of Northwich waterworks behind it. *B E Morrison*

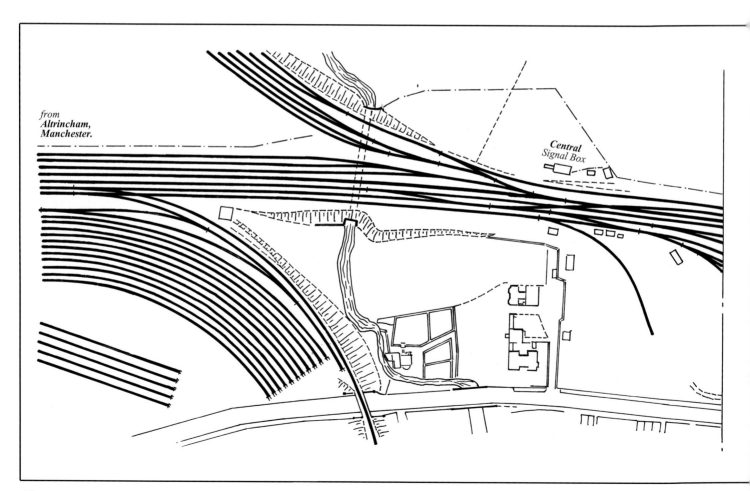

Northwich, c. 1924: A study in elegance as GCR Class '2' 4-4-0 No. **709** gets away with a Manchester service. Introduced in 1887, these distinctive machines worked Manchester - Kings Cross expresses before the opening of the GCR's London Extension, after which they were deployed on secondary services. Northwich had four, including No. 709, by 1921 but they were replaced by 'C13' tanks in 1930 whilst No. 709 was withdrawn in 1932. The first two coaches are CLC six wheelers from the 1890s, followed by twelve wheeled vehicles of 1887 vintage. *E Mason - R W Miller Collection*

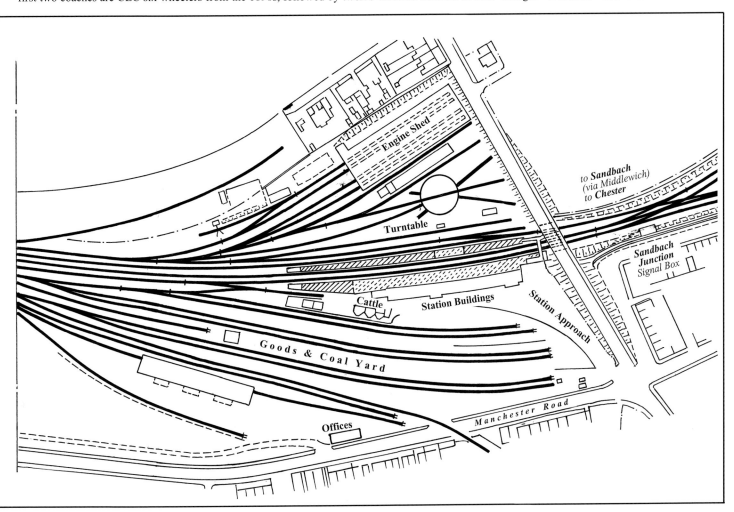

Barons Quay

Barons Quay, c. 1948: Photographs of Salt Branch No. **3** are virtually non existent, but 'J10' No. **5166** is seen shunting Moore and Brock's builder's yard at the end of the branch. Opened on 17th December 1867 after much agitation from local salt producers and the Weaver Trustees who wished to ship coal into Northwich for onward delivery by rail, it also served Barons Quay Mine and Ashton's Works, both derelict by 1940. Traffic from the Terracotta Brick Works had ceased by 1950, and the final customers were Moore and Brocks and Littler's timber yard after coal traffic to Northwich Gas Works ceased in 1953. The line closed in 1955 and had been lifted by 1959. *J C Lewis*

Northwich, 19th March 1966: A repeated spectacle of the 'Fifties and 'Sixties as an expertly handled Northwich '8F' storms away from the down yard with a typically heavy freight, taking a run at the 1 in 100 climb 'over the arches' to Hartford. No. **48408** takes the 0755 to Dee Marsh on an atmospheric spring morning, as No. **48398** comes 'on shed' and No. **44658** prepares to return to Crewe double heading the 0758 to Silverdale, Victoriana still predominates - CLC signals, water column and brazier, with the shed shearlegs completing the scene. *A Wilkinson*

(Above) **Northwich, c. 1959:** An unrebuilt 'Patriot' stands in the Up platform with the evening Crewe - Manchester parcels. On the shed, the 'Directors' have gone and Midland '3F' and '4F' 0-6-0s have largely replaced the 'J10s' on lighter work, but it is still some two or three years before the remaining LNER locomotives disappear completely. ICI's Lostock Works and the extensive up and down yards dominate the horizon, whilst Central Cabin, opened in 1896 and abolished on 30th March 1980, may be glimpsed through the shearlegs, with Northwich East box in the far distance. *D E Chatfield*

(Right) **Northwich Down island platform shelter, 26th September 1966.** Alas, this fine Victorian construction was about to be replaced with a functional 'shelter' which has since had to be much improved and rebuilt. *BR-LMR*

Northwich
Station

Northwich, 26th September 1966. The impressive exterior and clock tower of the 1897 station at Northwich. The extent of the buildings reflected the position of Northwich as one of the main traffic centres on the CLC. Today, only a small part of the building remains in use, but it is still basically complete.

BR-LMR

(Right) The large 'port cochere' reflected the days of gracious travel by horse and carriage. Later it was useful for handling parcels traffic and for accommodating the 'horses' of the 1960's. **BR-LMR**

Northwich Station
(September 1966)

(Below) The Booking Hall interior, a traditional look still prevailing at the time. The 'Fifties and 'Sixties corporate styles of signage and fittings never intruded on the overall scene.

(Centre-right) Northwich Up platform. The intricately detailed ironwork of the platform canopy is much in evidence, as is the now long vanished traffic in the shape of substantial parcel consignments and mailbags. **BR-LMR (3)**

(Right) **Northwich Station, 2nd April 1964.** Looking towards Sandbach Junction, a Class 108 DMU has just departed for Chester. The Middlewich Branch curves off to the left. Passengers await the next service to Manchester and there are three off-duty railwaymen to complete the scene.

Graham Whitehead

(Right) Northwich, view towards Chester, 22nd June 1964. Sandbach Junction Box peers beneath the Middlewich Road bridge. On the left, the signals control the exit from the Up and Down through road to Middlewich and Chester respectively. This was the line used by the Crewe motor trains until their withdrawal from 4th January 1960. Electric station lights had to wait until 1967. The 'careful' siting of the water column should be noted. **BR-LMR**

(Below-centre) Northwich Station Booking Office interior, c. 1964. Ticket racks and ledger books point to a bygone age in this era of 'APTIS', machines and their more recent successors! **BR-LMR**

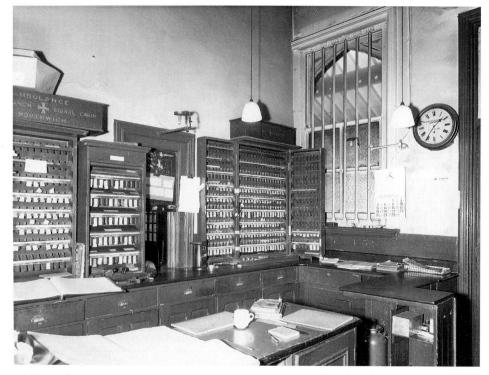

(Above) Station Master, British Railways c. 1960: Mr E Wrathall was the highly respected S.M. at Northwich from 1945-60. A time served railwayman, he began his career in the Control Office at Woodley in 1915, followed by a long period of 'trouble shooting' operating appointments at Liverpool, coming to Northwich during World War II to sort out the chaotic yard conditions. "Don't lie to me" he is said to have told an erring signalman. "Tell me what happened and I will go to Liverpool and do the lying for you"! At the age of 90, this remarkable railwayman was still able to provide clear and concise information for this volume. **A Wilkinson Collection**

Best-Kept Station

(Left) From 1948, Northwich Station won a prize in the Best-Kept Station Competition for three years running. The proud staff are: *Top*: H K McFall; *Centre*: E Wrathall (Station Master) and J Nutton. *Front*: S Plumb, T Woodier (Foreman) and A Bailey. In 1953, the date of the picture, a special prize was awarded by the Liverpool (C L) District.

G K Fox collection

The BR Era Dawns, c. 1949: Mature locomotives dominate this post-war scene 'J10' No. **65169** - still around in 1960 - is being coaled, alongside are a 'Pom Pom' 0-6-0, a 'Director', an 'L3' 2-6-4 tank and another 'J10' No. **65158**, with the shed's venerable breakdown train in the foreground. Modernity is represented by an '01' 2-8-0, but there are no '8F's yet and the 'J10s' still rule - just. The coal stage was enlarged during the war, the coaling crane coming second hand from Walton MPD in 1943, and there were some improvements to the yard facilities and ashpits at this time. *N R Knight*

NORTHWICH MOTIVE POWER DEPOT   1863 - 1984

With the opening of the railway in 1863, locomotives came from a depot at Knutsford, situated on the down side, north of the station. There was a turntable and servicing siding in the goods yard at Northwich, known for years afterwards as the 'Turntable Road', but the opening of the Helsby line and salt branches in 1869/70 saw the provision of a two road shed on the down side opposite the station. By 1877 this had expanded to four roads and had absorbed the work of Knutsford depot. The turntable was still in the goods yard, but by 1892 the shed had its own 45 foot table, replaced in 1902 by a 50 foot example from Trafford Park.

In 1879 four class '24' 2-4-0s worked the passenger trains, and by 1886 there were four '12A' and '24' 2-4-0s, together with one '60' class and nine '23' 0-6-0s for freight. Three passenger diagrams took No 57 to Manchester, Flixton and Irlam, No. 264 to Chester, Glazebrook and Manchester, and another 2-4-0 to Chester and Manchester. No. 264 and her crew were away for 13 1/2 hours - flexible rostering indeed! As early as 1868 it was already necessary to provide a pilot for the salt branches, and by 1870 there were three, working also at Winsford and Winnington. The mid 'Eighties found the freight locomotives working most-

ly within the CLC system; class '60' No. 459 went to Wigan (CLC) via Skelton Junction before working an afternoon passenger to Cuddington. No.142 worked to Godley Junction, whilst No. 27 took the overnight goods to Manchester Central - a train which still ran in 1937. Five other duties went to Helsby, Cuddington and Winnington. The local pilots were No.110 which shunted Northwich Yard and Salt Branches 1 and 2 0430-0830hrs, No.120 the 'Salt Pilot' from 0530-2000 (presumably Northwich yard and No. 3 Salt Branch), and No. 138 which worked to Winnington. Five 0-6-0s were sub-shedded at Helsby, Winsford and Chester, whilst Foreman T Chadwick - whose family was to provide generations of footplatemen - had 21 drivers and 22 firemen under his control.

Until the Edwardian years, most of the freight work was done by Sacre class '18' 0-6-0s of very modest dimensions - 140lbs pressure and only 12,897lbs tractive effort! '9A' ('N4') 0-6-2 tank No.173 was at the depot in 1894, and by 1905 there were five '9Cs' ('N5s') for yard shunting and trip work. The prevailing passenger allocation probably included some Scare '12A' 2-4-0s and Parker 'F1' 2-4-2 tanks, whilst the shed occasionally had new'C13' and

Women cleaners at Northwich Shed, c. 1916: The original shed site was in the station goods yard, but this was replaced in 1872 by a depot to the east of the station which was to remain open until 1984. For years the shed housed many old locomotives superannuated from the main line, but what was lacking in modernity was more than compensated for by the tradition of hard running and team spirit amongst the staff. Here, women cleaners are hard at work on class '9D' ('J10') 0-6-0 No. **644** during the First World War. The ladies brought a welcome improvement in staff facilities at the shed, paid for by the Government! The engine was the last round top firebox '9D', built at Gorton in 1893 and withdrawn ins 1938 as LNER No **5644**. 'J9s' and 'J10s' provided the shed's basic motive power for the next forty years. ***T Booth collection***

'C14' tanks on temporary loan from Gorton for running in purposes, one such visitor in 1907 being 'C14' No. 1120 shortly before being permanently allocated to Neasden. However, the first twenty years of the present century saw the area flooded with Parker '9B' ('J9') 0-6-0s, indeed in 1921 the shed had all but four of the class, twenty-seven in all. Several 'J10' 0-6-0s were also allocated, a major influx arriving from Retford when many 'J9s' were sent to Scotland in the mid 'Twenties.

From about 1873, the shed was host to Midland Railway locomotives sub-shedded from Manchester, which worked the limestone trains from Tunstead. In 1916, the incumbents were class '2' 0-6-0s Nos. 3171/2/6 which occupied No. 4 road, much to the chagrin of the CLC staff who had a much larger allocation to look after on the three remaining tracks. Other Midland engines worked in on general goods work from Heaton Mersey and coal trains from Yorkshire, including the 'Flat Iron' 0-6-4 tanks. In the 'Twenties the '2Fs' were replaced with '3F' and '4F' 0-6-0s, and in 1938 by Stanier '8Fs' with their Hopper trains, but it is a pity that the 1936 proposal to work the limestone traffic with two 'Garratts' did not materialise!

The pre-Grouping shed scene must have been quite colourful, the maroon livery of Midland and North Staffordshire locomotives contrasting with the green GCR colours of the native allocation, and the blackberry black of the LNWR locomotives which frequently used the turntable in between trips on the Middlewich branch. In 1922 the shed had six 'D6' 4-4-0s, twenty-seven 'J9s' and two 'J10s', some being outstationed at Helsby and Winsford. Three 'F1' tanks had just departed having worked main line passenger turns and the Winsford branch. The 4-4-0s had four passenger diagrams, mostly to Manchester and Irlam, and were rarely seen at Chester. These graceful machines departed in 1930, and two 'F1s' returned in 1928/9 for the Winsford service, being replaced in July 1929 by the brand new Sentinel railcar No. 602, but the line was beyond salvation and the railcar departed for Brunswick eighteen months later. The introduction of the Sentinel saw the closure of Winsford shed with the goods workings rearranged to be covered from Northwich, which also absorbed the duties of Helsby depot which was closed in the same year. Meanwhile at Northwich, turntable use had increased by 160% since 1900, and the existing fifty foot table needed extension rails for the largest locomotives, which in turn fouled the coaling road where up to 100 tons of coal were being handled daily. Despite the gloomy economic outlook in 1925, the CLC sensibly installed a new seventy foot vacuum turntable by Ransomes and Rapier, together with improved coaling facilities at a cost of some £4900.

Tank engines dominated the passenger work in the 'Thirties, mostly 'C13s', but with the 'N5s' increasingly involved once several had gained steam heating. The twenty-four engines at the shed in the Autumn of 1936 consisted of three 'C13s', nine 'N5s', eleven 'J10s' and the last 'J9' No. 5743; freight still being at a low ebb after the Depression of 1929-31. A popular arrival in 1938 was 'C14' No. 6121, a strong machine which departed with the 'C13s' in 1940, much to the disgust of the enginemen who were distinctly unimpressed with the replacements, ex GNR 'C12s', dubbed 'Minnies' in view of their 'breathless' performances! 'J10' 0-6-0s monopolised the freight service for fifteen years after the last 'J9' was withdrawn in 1936, and tackled almost anything, passenger or freight, despite the ever increasing traffic.

The Second World War brought extreme pressure on the facilities at this small depot. The allocation nearly doubled from 25 to 47 locomotives, with an increase in footplate staff from 110 to 160. Large numbers of repairs had to be transferred to other depots and there was much congestion on basic servicing facilities. In 1943, £6000 was spent in lengthening the ashpit and inspection pits, improving the yard layout and providing a further shed exit from the turntable to the outside carriage siding. Typically some 99 tons of LNER ash and 11 tons of LMS ash was deposited weekly at this time.

....*continued on page 52*

8
E

'Directors'

Roof replacement, 3rd June 1951: The original pitched roof is being replaced with LMS style precast concrete sections and 'D10' No. **62655** *The Earl of Kerry* is being washed out in the open. In the cab are boilermaker Fred Wilkinson and his mate Bill Keen. Leaning on the cab is boilerwasher D Evans, and to his left is Fitter Ken Dodd accompanied by Messrs E Bebbington, Frank Hope, J Humphries and Wilf Hopkins, many of whom were still at the shed when it closed to steam seventeen years later. The 'Directors' arrived in 1947 to replace the last 'D6' and 'D9' 4-4-0s, being replaced in turn by the later 'D11' 'Directors' between 1953 and 1955.

T Lewis courtesy N E Preedy

'Siesta', August 1955: Despite the layers of grime No. **62664** *Princess Mary* looks every inch a classic pre-Grouping express locomotive as she reposes in the remarkably clean coaling stage. The shed was then well known for its 'Directors', but the last three Nos. 62663/4/9 disappeared in the Spring of 1958 to work out their time in the Sheffield area. Although fairly slow off the mark, they were well liked by the enginemen who knew exactly how to exploit their speed capacity.

B E Morrison

Northwich, 'Forties Style'

Northwich, 14th September 1947: By 1877 the shed had been enlarged to a four road, gable roofed building which was becoming quite decrepit by the end of the CLC era. 'D10' 4-4-0 No. 2652 *Edwin A Beazley* stands outside the original shed building, the section to the right being reserved for the use of visiting LMS locomotives. The Shedmaster at the time was A. J. Somers who went on to a distinguished career on the Eastern Region and in retirement on the Festiniog Railway. *B W L Brooksbank*

continued from page 50

The shed was often critically short of capable passenger locomotives. In 1940-42 the 'C12s' predominated, followed by a batch of eight 'F1' and 'F2' tanks. In 1941, 'D6' No. 5865 arrived, followed in 1942 by No. 5859 and for the next sixteen years the shed was rarely without a venerable four coupled express locomotive. After 1943, the two 'D6s' shared the passenger diagrams with 'N5' tanks, indeed the three steam heater 'N5s' No's 5528/5911/29 must have had all the passenger work after the 'D6s' were transferred away at the end of 1945. Mercifully 'C13s' returned in the Spring of 1946, but were soon replaced by three 'D6s' and two 'D9' 4-4-0s. The increasing weight of trip workings to Winnington and demands for banking to Hartford saw a trial with a NER 'A7' 4-6-2 tank in 1939, followed by the arrival of two 'L1' (L3) 2-6-4 tanks No's. 5274 and 5343 in 1943. The 'J10' allocation was supplemented by two GNR 'J3' 0-6-0s in 1942/3, and two GER 'J67' tanks stayed for three months in early 1943. The war years also saw a great variety of visiting locomotives because of the vast output of ICI and the use of the CLC as an alternative route to the Mersey ports. 'USA' 2-8-0s worked in from Crewe quite frequently, whilst a great variety of freight power in addition to the usual GCR types was to be seen, including NER 0-8-0's.

The motive power position improved somewhat in 1946/7 when two 'J11' "Pom Poms" arrived, followed in August 1947 by the first batch of 'D10' 'Directors' to replace the 'D9s', and to pension off the last two surviving 'D6s' No's. 2101/6 in December. At Nationalisation the shed had three 'D10s'. eighteen 'J10s', one 'J11', two 'L3' and four 'N5' tanks, augmented by a further 'J11' and one 'C13' when absorbed into London Midland Region stock on 28th November 1948. For years, Northwich men had worked with old and underpowered locomotives, indeed the average age of the allocation in 1947 was 46 years. The skills acquired in coaxing these veterans around were certainly applied with a vengeance in the 'Fifties when the shed did get modern

locomotives, and with the '8Fs' ICI was able to claim that the 'Hoppers' were 'amongst the heaviest and fastest trains in the country, often running at 70mph' - this was frequently not too far from the truth! The passing of time had also taken its toll on the shed buildings, for in 1950 the gabled roof was replaced with pre-cast concrete flat roof of the latest LMS pattern.

Until 1950, the shed was coded NTH under the LNER scheme, then briefly 13D until the Trafford Park district was absorbed by Longsight in May, and then 9G until April 1958. Finally part of the Edge Hill district, the shed was '8E' until closure to steam in March 1968. The arrival of the sheds' first Stanier '8F' No. 48340 from Perth in April 1949, saw the 'Hopper' diagrams transferred to Northwich and by 1950 there was an allocation of ten. Contemporary arrivals were '4F' and '3F' 0-6-0s for the Middlewich pilot and heavier trip workings on which they replaced the popular and versatile 'J11s' by 1953, the 'celebrities' at this time being the 'L3' tanks and 'Director' 4-4-0s. 'L3' No. 69062 disappeared in 1951, being replaced by tender cab 'Super D' 0-8-0 No. 49435, one of several acquired in the early 'Fifties. Never popular, they were frequently stored serviceable in between fitful appearances on the 'Trippers', but they did eventually gain a regular mineral turn to Cheadle. The arrival of Crewe South diesel shunters in 1952/3 ended the 'N5' allocation, and with more LMS and LNER 2-8-0's available, especially after the Woodhead electrification, the 'J10' allocation became a mere handful for the Winsford, Chester, Skelton and local trip workings. The last 'L3' tank, No. 69052 disappeared in 1954, and by 1955 the heavy trips T55 and T56, introduced in 1953 between Northwich and the new yards at Oakleigh and Gorstage were usually worked by double shifted '8F's'.

In the early post war years, Northwich men did not usually get past Glazebrook, Warrington CLC, Helsby, Dee Marsh and Godley Junction, occasionally venturing to Sheffield or Wrexham ....*continued on page 54*

Scenes on Shed

Sunday Morning Congregation, 3rd March 1963: The freight service was still 100% steam, and although ex LNER types have finally disappeared, large numbers of '8Fs', 'Black Fives' and 'WD' 2-8-0s await the steamraiser's attention later in the day. Also allocated were '4Fs' and BR Class '2s' for trip working and LMS and BR 350HP diesels based at Crewe which had been yard shunting since 1953. The shearlegs still dominate the scene, but were not often used by this time.

D L Chatfield

Replenishment, 9th October 1965: Having been coaled and watered, Wakefield 'WD' No. **90404** moves off the coaling stage amidst the broken bric a brac of the last years of steam - standards of tidiness were not what they had been only a few years before! The engine had worked in via Standedge with Yorkshire coal from Woolley Colliery. In the background is the chimney for the sand furnace - an essential piece of equipment at all steam freight depots.

A Wilkinson

Northwich MPD - 8E

Stoical Survivors, 25th February 1968: With just one week to go before closure to steam, Stanier '8Fs' monopolise the shed yard, whilst sad lines of withdrawn sisters are stored in the goods yard in the background. Arriving from Perth in April 1949, No **48340** was the first '8F' to be allocated to Northwich, serving with distinction for most of the intervening period before escaping with No **48727** - alongside - for further service at Rose Grove until the end of steam working in August. Grand work was still being coaxed out of the run down fleet, but there will not be too much more hard labour for the crews with the long rake and chisel bar in the foreground.

A Wilkinson

Consolidation Country, c. 1961: A view across the shed front shows a mixture of LMS and LNER 2-8-0s which had finally ousted the 'J10' 0-6-0s by 1960. Two rebuilt '04s' Nos **63895** and **63905** of Gorton are on view, together with the inevitable '8Fs', No **48403** nearest the camera, is standing on one of the two westernmost roads reserved before nationalisation for LMS locomotives sub shedded from Heaton Mersey for coal and limestone traffic - a cause of some contention to the CLC staff who had little enough room for their own allocation of 30 or so locomotives.   *J F Ward Collection*

continued from page 52...........................
with a pilotman. Four sets of LMS men, supplemented when necessary from Heaton Mersey, worked the 'Hoppers', becoming part of the Northwich establishment in 1950. In the 'Fifties there were six Links:- No.1 Passenger, No.2 Goods, No.3 Hoppers, No.4 'Spiv' (Rest Day Relief), No.5 Pilot Link to Winsford, Chester and Skelton, and No.6 Shed Link. In 1954, No.1 Link had eleven weekly turns, 0813 return Hoppers to Tunstead, 1910 Heaton Mersey, 0535 Passenger, 1245 Hoppers, 0610 Skelton (relieved at midday by No.2 Link travelling out on the 1329 from Northwich), 1900 Passenger, 1735 Passenger, 1430 Dee Marsh, 0435, 1615 and 1000 Passengers respectively, some of these being relieving turns to Manchester or Chester at Northwich. The final week of the twelve week roster was in the 'Spiv' Link, covering the Rest Days of the Passenger Link. In 1955 Wilf Egerton fired eighteen '8Fs', two 'N5s', three 'J10s', five 'D10s', three '04s', two '3Fs', two 'Compounds', two 'Super Ds', two WDs', three BR '5MTs', one '3MT' Stanier tank, one '4MT' tank and one 'Jubilee' No. 45618 in this link, so there was plenty of variety!

In 1958, No. 2 Goods Link worked the 1140 Warrington CLC, 0425 Chester pickup, 1900 Saltney (via Hooton or Helsby LNW), 0329 Glazebrook, Spiv Week, 0230 and 0220 Dee Marsh on respective weeks. Typically, one 'J10', four 'J39s', fourteen '8Fs', six '04s', and one Fowler tank No. 42319 were encountered by Wilf in this link. When first set up in 1950, the Hopper link went only from Winnington to Tunstead, but two weeks work on the Winnington and Winsford trips were soon added.

The Yard Pilot diagrams before dieselisation reveal just what a busy place Northwich was; No.1 Pilot (usually 'J10' No. 65202) shunted the station yard and Barons Quay branch, being treble shifted from 0145hrs. No. 2 'Top End' Pilot (N5 No.69262), treble shifted, shunted the Up yard, banked to Knutsford or Hartford, and double headed a trip to Helsby. No.3 'Top End' Pilot, a treble shifted 'N5' or 'J10' worked the up yard, whilst No.4 'Top End' Pilot, two turns, ('J10' No. 5174) worked the east end of the down yard and transferred traffic to the up yard. No.5 Pilot, a treble shifted 'J10', covered the down yard. Until 1953, the tremendously strong and noisy 'L3' tanks, treble shifted, banked from Winnington up to Hartford Sidings, never venturing onto main line work and only occasionally reaching Northwich. They did well on the 1 in 53 up from Winnington, but tales were told of crews baling out in the opposite direction to avoid an involuntary dip in the River Weaver which miraculously never happened!

During 1955, the shed became the final home for the 'D10' 'Directors', the last, No. 62653 *Sir Edward Fraser* being withdrawn in October. The later 'D11' 'Directors' continued to work the passenger trains, supplemented by a small allocation of LM 2-6-4 tanks following the occasional loan of such locomotives from Crewe North some years earlier. By 1957, the 'J10' allocation had dwindled to four, with '3F' and '4F' 0-6-0s predominant on the lighter work. In the spring of 1958, the shed lost its last four 'Directors'. They had been stored at Trafford Park for a while, and went to Sheffield to work out their time, being replaced briefly by four Stanier 2-6-4 tanks with the Fowler variety very successfully predominating for three years until full dieselisation in 1961. Derby 'Lightweight' class 108 DMUs were progressively introduced on the passenger diagrams from 1959, and the last Fowler tanks disappeared in October 1961, although the Shed did briefly acquire a Stanier class '3' tank No. 40086 for two months during the summer. Early in 1959, the Midland '3F' 0-6-0s moved on, leaving 'J10' No. 65169 as the last GCR locomotive at the depot surviving until January 1960. Two new 'babies', BR class '2' 2-6-0s Nos. 78038/57, arrived in November 1959 and were theoretically supplemented by Midland '2F' No. 58120 for three months in the following summer. By early 1961, the allocation stood at thirty-six; eight Fowler tanks, three '4Fs'. twenty-two '8Fs', and three BR 2MTs. The '4Fs disappeared in the Autumn of 1964 having lost the Middlewich Pilot turn in 1962 and much of their main line work to '8Fs'. An Ivatt class '2' No. 46472 arrived in 1963, one of several of this class to be allocated over the next few years for the trips to Chester, Winsford, Knutsford and Marston. In November 1964, BR class '3' 2-6-0s Nos. 77011/4 arrived for this work.

By this time the shed's locomotives and men were getting a much wider range of work. From the mid 'Fifties they began to work to Saltney via Helsby or Hooton with transfers for the Western Region, and from 1957 came jobs to Stoke and later Uttoxeter. The CLC route to Warrington became less well used, and latterly all trains in this direction were via the LNWR lines to Warrington, Clock Face and Ravenhead. From about 1964, Northwich men also began working to Carnforth and sometimes Carlisle with the Soda ash jobs to Whitehaven and Larbert, and by 1965 there were turns to Silverdale and a new trip working to Winsford and Over for the developing rock salt traffic inaugurated in 1966. Officially, most locomotive diagrams remained relatively short out and home turns to Godley Junction, Dewsnap, Gowhole, Peak Forest, Dee Marsh, and the Warrington area, but a Northwich '8F' was booked to Carlisle with the Larbert train and the I030 Whitehaven locomotive worked right through. It was not unusual to see Northwich engines working across the Pennines to Yorkshire with coal empties or to Carlisle via a variety of routes having been 'borrowed' by the authorities whilst working into the Manchester area. In these last few years of steam working, the shed had a staff of approximately 80 drivers, 20 passed firemen, 57 firemen and 36 maintenance staff.

From 1963/4, the basic '8F' allocation stood at around 15-20 and they handled the whole of the freight service. However, in 1963 the indifferent Metrovik Co-Bo type 2 diesels were tried on the 'Hoppers', a prelude to successful trials with BR Sulzer Type 2s which saw the service handed over to these. Longsight supplied diesels from the summer of 1964. However, for the next $3^{1/2}$ years the remainder of the freight service remained steam worked and the '8Fs' turned their hand to all manner of trains including parcels and occasional excursion workings. Until 1967 there was still a demand for smaller locomotives on the Winsford, Knutsford and Marston pilots. The BR class 3's disappeared from this work in 1966. No. 77011 was withdrawn in February, whilst No. 77014 was transferred in April to Guildford of all places! Various Ivatt Class '2' 2-6-0s arrived as replacements from March 1966, but were withdrawn in May 1967 by which time only the Mouldsworth and Knutsford jobs remained. Throughout 1967, the shed's 19 '8Fs' soldiered on, many falling by the wayside with relatively minor defects, being replaced by battle weary survivors ousted from other depots by the inevitable march of dieselisation. There had never been a surfeit of cleaners at Northwich, and the '8Fs' seemed particularly neglected, although performance apparently suffered very little! From the Autumn of 1967, English Electric Type 4 diesels began to take over, and it fell to a select trio of '8Fs' Nos. 48036, 48272, and 48632 to see out just over 100 years of steam working from the depot on Saturday 2nd March 1968.

For the next sixteen years the shed continued as a signing on and stabling point until final closure at the end of November 1984. By this time it was the only surviving CLC shed building, and possessed three diesel refuelling tanks mounted on

'Running' Repairs

'All Strung up', 1955: No self respecting Great Central engine shed was ever without a shearlegs for lifting locomotives, although very few of them were under cover! The CLC followed suit at Northwich where the 'Directors' were often hoisted for attention to bogies, axleboxes or valve examinations. Here, No. **62653** *Sir Edward Fraser*, the last of the 'D10s', is seen some two months before withdrawal as a D11' prepares to move 'off shed' in the background.

B E Morrison

Men of steam, February 1968: The Northwich shed staff pose in front of a typically filthy '8F' in the last weeks of steam. *Top Row L to R - Fitters Mate* Dennis Hobson, *Ashman* Fred Worrall, *Boilermaker* Fred Wilkinson, *Boilerwasher* George Daniels. *Middle Row - Fitter* Peter Yould, *Fitters Mate* Cyril Atherton, *Fitter* Ken O'Dowd, *Fitters Mate* Glyn Jones, *Boilerwasher* Tom Terry. *Bottom Row - Driver* Alf Washington, *Fitter* Ken Dodd, *Boilermakers Mate* Bill Keen, *Fitters Mate* Eric Bebbington, *Fitter* Eddie Watts, *Shed Foreman* Eric Varty, *Foreman Fitter* Bill (Nobby) Johnson, *Firelighter* Clarry France, *Ashman* Ernie Rimmer, *Fitters Mate* Harold Robinson, *Boilermakers Mate* Frank Hope. **Their life was no sinecure in the harsh environment of a locomotive shed in all weathers - as many preservationists have since found out!** *W Egerton Collection*

ancient underframes, one of which came from an LNWR 'Bloomer' 2-2-2 tender and was eventually preserved. In the early 'Seventies the turntable was removed and the shed lay-out modified accordingly. Motive power was supplied by the North Western Lines pool and grand work was done by the Sulzer Class '25s' on the 'Hoppers' until their rather unsuc-cessful replacement by pairs of class '20s' early in 1984. Hence it was a mixture of classes '25', '47', '40' and '20' which saw out the Depot's final years. Operations were drastically rationalised by then: The ICI trip workings were reduced to one diagram which disappeared in 1982 together with all the yard pilots, whilst the remaining traffic was reorganised around fewer, but larger bulk workings. The 'Hoppers' final-ly became the responsibility of Buxton depot, although with respectable head end power in the form of paired Class '37s'.

A happy interlude in the 'Eighties was the return of steam power to the Depot for the Liverpool and Manchester Railway 150th Anniversary. For some years afterwards, under the auspices of the '8E Association', the shed was able to play host to numerous steam locomotives on special work-ings, and it is thoroughly regrettable that protracted unneces-sary obstacles sadly prevented an '8F' from returning to the Depot before demolition in the Spring of 1991.

Redundant assets, 25th February 1968: Victorian fittings from the steam age - such as this CLC water column and brazier - had become increasingly care-worn by the late 'Sixties. The BR Sulzer Type '2s' appeared on the Hoppers' in 1964, and from 1967 English Electric Type '4s' took over the remaining workings. No. **48036** has just one week of service left and the domination of the diesel will soon be complete. *A Wilkinson*

Steam Finale

Grand Finale, 2nd March1968: Driver Clarry Egerton and Fireman Jeff Elmes prepare to take No. **48632** 'off shed' for her final afternoon's work on the Winnington Tripper on the last day of steam. With No. **48036** on the Wallerscote Tripper in the hands of Driver Ken Bate and Fireman Bob Cummings, the running was in the very best businesslike Northwich tradition, indeed some of the 'rockets' may still be in orbit! These efforts inspired the preservation of No. 8233 on the Severn Valley Railway where she often carries an honorary '8E' shedplate.   *A Wilkinson*

Northwich, Sandbach Junction, 22nd June 1964. A view in the Up direction looking towards Northwich Station. The crossover in the foreground is from the Middlewich Branch, and the access from the Up and Down through road was abolished with the opening of the Hartford power box in 1980. Today, access to the Middlewich Branch is east of the station. Also just visible through the right hand opening is the wartime connection from the MPD via the Outside Carriage Road..

BR-LMR

Sandbach Junction, December 1966: This attractive 40 lever CLC box was the second on the site, opening in 1886 and closing with the full commissioning of the Hartford Power Box on 30th March 1980. Prompt action by Signalman George Griffiths prevented a disaster in August 1949 when a brake van and 43 wagons ran away from Cuddington. Running at 45 - 50mph they were miraculously diverted past the 1705 to Manchester, 1707 to Chester and 1710 to Crewe standing in the station, and Signalman Jack Elm at Central Cabin was able to find a clear siding in the Down yard. Guard Harold Worth stuck to his post and was even able to wave at passengers as he passed by! A runaway coal train from Middlewich in 1910 did collide with empty stock in the station with dramatic results. On a calmer note, '8F' No. **48324** approaches with Runcorn - Worksop empties.   *A Wilkinson*

The Northwich "Triangle"

Sandbach Junction, 28th March 1967: In the 'Fifties and 'Sixties, the Victorian terraces bounding the Northwich triangle frequently resounded to the stentorian bark of hard worked Stanier '8Fs', and No. **48631** is seen forging away with a typically heavily loaded Wallerscote tripper of 'Covhops'. The 'Covhops', a familiar sight in the area for many years, were introduced in 1952 for caustic soda and other bulk chemicals. Also from the mid 'Fifties, two double shifted '8Fs' powered the trips to Gorstage (for Wallerscote) and Oakleigh (for Winnington), together with banking to Hartford North.

Sandbach Junction, West, 11th June 1965: Nearing the end of the "Crab" allocation at Gorton, Horwich 2-6-0 No. **42715** leaves Northwich with coal from West Yorkshire for John Summer's steelworks at Shotton. The chord line from the Middlewich branch trails in from the right, with the cabin housing the miniature token instruments for the single line visible by the telegraph pole. The footbridge in the background was the first CLC pre stressed concrete structure dating from 1922, but was replaced in 1997.
A Wilkinson

Sandbach Junction, South, 11th June 1965: BR Class '4' 4-6-0 No. **75020** approaches with the 0840 Crewe - Northwich pick up. On the right is the south to west chord, planned in the LNWR Bill of 1865, but not actually opened until 16th June 1957 in response to increasing petroleum traffic from the Wirral to the East and West Midlands, and to facilitate diversions from the West Coast Main Line. *A Wilkinson*

Royle Street Crossing, 11th June 1965: Freshly outshopped from Crewe, '8F' No. **48650** curves on to the Middlewich branch with the 0840 transfers for Basford Hall. These 'salt expresses' were usually the stronghold of '4Fs' and 'Super D' 0-8-0s, but latterly '8Fs' and 'Black Fives', although being worked by Crewe, anything was possible. The Crewe trippers continued until the partial closure of Basford Hall in 1972, after which much of Northwich's non trainload output went via Warrington. *A Wilkinson*

Sandbach Junction, West, 19th March 1966: '8F' No. **48118** comes gingerly down the 1 in 100 from Hartford and off the mist shrouded Weaver viaduct past the site of Cemetery Crossing, slowing to take the Middlewich chord with Runcorn - Beeston empties. It is rumoured that one Northwich driver purloined a 1 in 100 gradient post to adorn the grave of his late wife in the nearby cemetery. A rare tribute indeed! *A Wilkinson*

Weaver Viaduct, 27th January 1968: With the Hartford East down distant off for the Winnington Branch, Type 2 diesel No. **D5279** manfully assisted by '8F' No. **48683**, is just about to reach the Weaver Viaduct on the 1 in 100/80 climb to Hartford North with the 1016 hoppers from Tunstead. Introduced in 1964, the class '25s' were worthy successors to the '8Fs' on these trains, especially as they regularly took two extra hoppers. They were unsuccessfully replaced by paired class '20s' in 1984, but before long paired class '37s' were used. With the closure of Northwich Depot in November 1984, the 'Hoppers' sadly became the preserve of Buxton Depot.
A Wilkinson

Weaver Viaduct

Weaver Viaduct, c. 1910: Two Weaver boats loaded with salt from Winsford come through Hunt's Lock as a Sacre '18' 0-6-0 stands at Hartford East's starter with an Up freight in this Edwardian scene on the 50 arch viaduct. These locomotives dated back to 1869 and moved much of the district's freight up to the First World War, being superseded by the '9B'/'9D' series (LNER 'J9'/'J10'). The insistence of the Weaver Trustees on a clearance of 69ft above the water provided Northwich with a dominant landmark, but at the price of a station some way from the town centre and delays in opening the West Cheshire Railway whilst the viaduct was completed.
T Booth Collection

The Lock & Viaduct, Northwich.

(Top) **Weaver Viaduct, 2nd January 1967:** Railway enthusiasts had no cause to regret the building of the viaduct, given the pyrotechnic displays from steam locomotives tackling its 1 in 100 gradient! Here '9F' No. **92012** blasting up the bank with Grange Junction - Ellesmere Port empty tanks meets '8F' No. **48693** accelerating away from Hartford East Junction with Hartford North (Oakleigh) - Woolley Colliery empties.

(Centre) **Hartford East Junction, 14th June 1967:** The box opened in October 1901 and closed on 21st December 1975, following Phase I of the commissioning of the new Hartford Power Box. Blowing off confidently, No. **48363** pounds up the bank with the heavy 1915 transfers for Warrington. The Winnington branch curves sharply away at 1 in 76/97 to Hartford North, the junction witnessing a serious accident on 7th October 1948 when due to a signalling error, Stoke '4F' No. **44448** going light to Northwich, met '8F' No. **48154** forging across the junction with Hoppers for Winnington.

(Left) **Hartford East Junction, 23rd January 1965:** The tall signalbox perched at the western end of the viaduct provided a wide panorama across the town and a grandstand view of hard worked locomotives climbing away from Northwich. No. **48631**, the Winnington trip engine, rattles the foundations as she trips Yorkshire coal from Northwich yard up to Oakleigh Sidings. *A Wilkinson(3)*

Hartford

Hartford North, 2nd January 1967: Driver Joe Mills brings No. **48151**, deputising for a failed diesel, round the sharp curve between Hartford East and North boxes, opened about 1907, with the 1016 Hoppers from Tunstead. No. **48643**, the Winnington trip engine, is banking at the rear. No. 48151 was one of the best '8Fs' at Northwich, moving to Woodham Brother's Barry scrapyard on withdrawal in December 1967. Restored to working order in 1987 by Mr J Smith, she has been favoured with numerous main line runs, but not alas with a set of Hoppers!

A Wilkinson

Hartford North, 15th June 1967: Driver Charlie Wright and Fireman Len Higgins have just brought No. **48100** and the 1030 Covhops for Whitehaven up the 1 in 116 from Oakleigh Sidings, and onto the western arm of the triangle towards Greenbank. Hartford North box on the right opened in 1904 and closed on 21st December 1975. Before the opening of Oakleigh, many more sidings existed in the triangle area.

A Wilkinson

Hartford Exchange

Hartford Exchange, 21st March 1953: Stanier Class '3' tank No. **40209** passes the signal box and still busy sidings with a Chester stopping train, whilst 'L3' 2-6-4 tank No. **69052** takes a break from shunting. The sidings here were largely superseded by Oakleigh Sidings later in the year, but the box remained open as a ground frame until 20th July 1968.   *N Fields*

Winnington

Winnington Branch, 17th February 1954: Replacements for the 'L3' tanks were two tender cab LNW 0-8-0s of which No. 49435 was the best. They were by no means popular and '8Fs' or the best '4F' No. 44456 were used whenever possible on the trip workings. By 1955 these trains between Oakleigh, Gorstage and Northwich demanded '8F' power anyway. Here No. **49435** is seen climbing away from Oakleigh towards Hartford North.

T K Widd

(Above-left) **Oakleigh Sidings, 2nd January 1967:** '9F' 2-10-0 No. **92137** gets away up the 1 in 116 to Hartford North with eastbound mineral empties.
A Wilkinson.

(Above-right) **Oakleigh Sidings, 2nd March 1968:** The sidings were laid out mostly on a gradient of 1 in 116 and '9F' No. **92218**, assisted by an ICI shunter, is having a rare struggle on greasy rails to start the 1030 to Whitehaven on the last day of steam working from Northwich. Gravel Pit sidings lie beyond the bridge in the background.
A Wilkinson.

Gravel Pit Sidings, c. 1950: This relatively small group of sidings was the starting point for many trains before the opening of Oakleigh, whilst capacity problems meant that other services had to be marshalled and started from the Hartford Triangle. The single track Winnington branch is on the right, with Beswicks Road box, closed in 1953, in the distance at the top of the final 1 in 53 down to Winnington and the River Weaver.

T Booth Collection

Winnington, 1913: Half way down the final bank, small ten ton wagons of coal and limestone provide a notable contrast with the 44ton capacity lime-stone hoppers of 1936, and the HAAs of the 1970s. The branch opened in June 1870 to serve Byeflat and Warboise salt works behind the fence on the right, but Brunner Mond's Winnington Works soon dominated matters after 1873. The round building in the centre is the CLC's Winnington and Anderton Goods Depot which remained open until 1969. Two Sacre '18' 0-6-0s are at work amongst the wagons. *ICI Chemicals & Polymers (Above and Below)*

James Watt at Winnington: Motive power at Winnington, Lostock and Wallerscote Works was mainly provid-ed by Borrows Well tanks of a very old design dating back to 1863. They came from Borrows from 1881 until 1912, and Kerr Stuart continued deliveries

until 1929 when about 25 were in service at the various Mid Cheshire works. After 1914, they were supplemented by 15 or so 0-4-0 saddletanks from various builders, but curiously ICI never departed from this wheel arrangement. *James Watt* went new to Winnington in 1886, moving to Buxton Lime Firms Ltd in 1923. Sister locomotives remained at Northwich until 1957, by which time some had acquired turbo generators and two way radios!

Oakleigh

Oakleigh Sidings, 21st February 1954: Originally, the Winnington branch was a sylvan byway between Hartford North and Gravel Pit Sidings, but in 1953 the area was opened out to form Oakleigh Sidings, new reception and departure roads for Winnington Works. 'L3' No. **69052** has just arrived with a trip working from Northwich. The empty hoppers awaiting return to Tunstead are standing on the original running line. After this date BR locomotives did not venture beyond Oakleigh to Gravel Pit and Winnington, this becoming ICI's domain.
T K Widd

(Left) **Brunel at Winnington, c. 1953:** Although ICI considered diesels in the 'Thirties, orders were placed at the end of the Second World War with Andrew Barclay for a further six steam locomotives. The chunky 0-4-0 design, vacuum fitted to work the limestone hoppers, is represented by *Brunel* delivered in 1948. Within nine years, ICI was fully dieselised

(Below) **Hartford North, May 1949.** Much trip-working and banking was necessary between Winnington, Gravel Pit Sidings, Hartford Sidings and Northwich, most of it beyond the capacity of a 'J10'. Between 1943 and 1954, GCR Class '1B' (LNER 'L3') freight tanks were employed quite succesfully on this work. They never ventured onto main line freights and only occasionally banked the 'Hoppers' from Northwich, although they did sometimes bank from Hartford East only, being stabled in the headshunt there. Their real forte was in pushing heavy trains up the 1 in 53 from Winnington before this became ICI territory in 1953. Here, No. **69062** nears Hartford North having worked up from Winnington.
P M Alexander, courtesy Millbrook House

Hartford and Greenbank

(Above) **Hartford and Greenbank, 20th April 1952:** 'D10' No. **62656** *Sir Clement Royds* arrives with the well patronised 1157 Manchester Central - Chester Northgate. The typical secondary platform shelter and distinctive CLC station nameboard are seen to good effect. Hartford Exchange box stands in the distance, whilst Greenbank box, opened in 1886 and replaced on 21st December 1975 by a new power box for the Northwich area, situated in the yard to the left, may be seen at end of the Up platform.   **H B Priestley**

(Centre) A 1961 view looking east towards Northwich.

Mowat Collection

Hartford, n.d; A later view, again looking east, with little change.

(Above) **Hartford and Greenbank, c. 1960:** Stanier 'Duchess' No. **46246** *City of Manchester* draws admiring glances as she drifts past the neat but functional West Cheshire Railway buildings with a diverted West Coast express heading for Crewe via the Northwich chord and Middlewich. The station buildings were very similar in plan to those of the Cheshire Midland east of Northwich, but at Delamere and Mouldsworth, rock faced stone was the building material. The station became 'Greenbank' from 7th May 1973 to avoid confusion with Hartford main line station. *R W Miller Collection*

(Right) **Hartford Junction CLC, 24th February 1968:** The distinctively tall CLC box and signals still make a brave show as Driver Eddy Brown brings No. **48493** sure footedly across the layout and onto the spur to Hartford LNW Junction with the heavy 1030 Whitehaven Covhops, loaded with soda ash for the Marchon Products plant at Corkickle. Steam had just two weeks to go, but the '8Fs' were still working through with this demanding duty, the crews being relieved at Carnforth. The signalbox, which provided a most impressive view of the junction opened in 1886, closing on 15th May 1976. *A Wilkinson*

(Left) **Hartford Junction, CLC, 21st March 1953:** Although designed for goods and shunting work, Parker's '9F' (LNER 'N5') 0-6-2 tanks of 1891 were extensively used on CLC passenger trains in the 'Thirties and 'Forties, and could still be seen on occasional turns from Chester as late as 1957. They had to be thrashed on such work, although No. **69281** appears to be coping well enough on this Chester service, despite the evidence of a burnt smokebox door! *N Fields*

Hodge Lane, 14th September 1954: Northwich '8F' No. **48521** has steam to spare on the long rise to Cuddington as she crosses the West Coast Main Line at Hartford with a mixed freight of steel and iron ore bound for John Summer's Steelworks at Dee Marsh. *P H Wells*

End of an era

Cuddington, 6th March 1948: The days of the 'J10s' on main line goods work were rapidly drawing to a close by the late 'Forties, but No. **5158** is blowing off merrily as she nears Cuddington after the demanding climb from Northwich with a down goods bound for Dee Marsh or Helsby. No doubt some careful artistry with the shovel will have been necessary to produce such a performance. *L&GRP, courtesy NRM*

Cuddington

(Below) **Cuddington, c. 1907:** A vintage scene as the Winsford branch goods, headed by a Sacre '18' 0-6-0 poses for the camera. These locomotives were introduced in 1868 for CLC goods traffic and Northwich had large numbers of them until replaced by the '9Ds' (LNER 'J9' & 'J10s') during the First World War. The sidings on the right were useful for 'staging' loads on the climb to Delamere or for splitting trains on the quite heavily graded Winsford branch. Heavy timber traffic for Messrs. Gardners Ltd. was also dealt with for many years, this being the eastern extremity of Delamere Forest. Latterly the sidings were used until the mid 'Sixties for stabling the stock of the Manchester - Cuddington commuter service. **A G Treves Collection, courtesy of R W Miller**

(Above) **Cuddington, c. 1931.** As well as providing a good three quarter view of the signal box, this 'Thirties photograph records the unusually shaped roof of the goods shed. It is interesting to note the logevity of the way in which CLC boxes retained their cabin name overlooking the running lines. Latterly, Cuddington also happened to be the western limit of maintenance of the District Signal & Telegraph Department based in Stockport. **G H Platt**

(Below) **Cuddington, c. 1952:** 'D10' 'Director' No. **62659** *Worsley Taylor* rolls into the platform with an afternoon train for Chester. The station buildings have been supplemented with a variety of wooden extensions housing the parcels office and lamp room, the ladies and general waiting rooms being in the main building. The nameboard still proclaims the station to be the junction for 'Whitegate and Winsford' some twenty years after the service finished! The signal-box, dating from 1885, closed on 15th November 1970, the station having closed to goods traffic on 2nd March 1964. **N R Knight**

Edwardian Delamere

Delamere: The buildings on both platforms follow the standard West Cheshire plan, but are in sandstone, not brick. To the left was a road access to the Up platform, constructed in 1911 to facilitate the heavy milk traffic to the creamery at Cuddington and to Manchester, which remained an important business well into the 'Fifties. *T Booth Collection*

(Left) **Delamere, c. 1926:** Robinson '9K' 4-4-2 tank (LNER 'C13') No. **310** still in Great Central livery, arrives with a Chester service. Built at Gorton in 1905, she became BR No. **67434**, being withdrawn in October 1957. The local sandstone favoured for construction purposes by the West Cheshire Company, is much in evidence in the sturdy overbridge and platform facings.
L Hobday, M Bentley Collection

(Below) **Delamere, 10th April 1959:** Single line working is in force to Mouldsworth following the derailment of a tank train on the down loop exit points. With Station Master Rodney Hampson of Mouldsworth acting as pilotman, Fowler tank No. **42417** goes 'wrong line' past the signalbox with a train for Chester. The complex - and expensively maintained! - pointwork on the right, leading into the goods yard, was characteristic of many West Cheshire stations. *N Jones*

Forest Interlude, 9th July 1966: '8F' No. **48057** tops the climb from Northwich to Delamere and gathers her train - a Northwich - Dee Marsh coal haul - for the descent at 1 in 90 through the heart of Delamere Forest. Delamere had closed to goods on 1st March 1965, but the loop and sidings were still used for staging heavy loads and part of a Trentham - Shotwick coal haul may be seen in the distance. The signalbox closed on 15th May 1976, but the sidings remained accessible until the removal of the ground frames by August 1980. The station yard has since become a visitor's centre for the forest. *B Sullivan/T Tomalin*

Delamere Forest

(Below) **Sylvan Solitude, 27th April 1954:** A delightful study of Ivatt tank No. **41234** topping the climb through the forest with a train for Manchester. These lively little machines were the first virtually new locomotives to be allocated to Chester Northgate and provided a welcome change from generations of 'N5s', 'C13s', and 'J10s' on the shed's passenger diagrams.

N Fields

Raising the echos, May 1949: Great Central '11B' (LNER 'D9') 4-4-0 No. **62330** tackles the gradient through the forest with the 0920 Chester Northgate - Manchester Central semifast. Introduced in 1901, the locomotives originally saw service on the GCR's London Extension, followed by use on a wide variety of secondary services before concentrating on the CLC from the mid 'Thirties to see out their final years. *P M Alexander/Millbrook House*

Mouldsworth

Mouldsworth, May 1949: This quiet country junction located in a homely setting surrounded by coniferous forests and sandstone outcrops was quite popular with photographers. 'D9' 4-4-0 No. **62305** - one of two allocated to Northwich at the time and last survivor when withdrawn in July 1950 - gets away with a Manchester stopping train. *P M Alexander/Millbrook House*

Mouldsworth, August 1958: '3F' 0-6-0 No. **43538** on the Chester - Northwich pick up is setting back onto its train having visited the Pooley weigh-bridge in the yard with a wagon of scrap metal from Chester Northgate. This traffic was weighed at Mouldsworth before onward despatch to the steel furnaces of Sheffield. Behind the engine was another weighbridge and loading plant for the Ship Canal Sand Company's quarry which opened about 1933. The quarry provided occasional loads of moulding sand, but domestic coal was the main traffic latterly until 1968. The trip did not venture beyond Mouldsworth after 1965. The Guard is telephoning the signalbox from the ground frame to let the signalman know that shunting operations have ceased for the day. The station closed to goods on 30th September 1968.
N Jones

'Home with the milk', 30th August 1958: Porter Eric Cowup unloads empty milk churns from Manchester at Mouldsworth for collection by local farmers. Milk traffic was still fairly significant at this time, but the daily milk trains and return empties from Chester to Manchester, a feature of the line for many years, no longer ran by this date.
N Jones

(Above) **Mouldsworth Junction, c. 1938:** Signalman William Jones amidst the immaculate surroundings of Mouldsworth box. His railway career spanned 49 years and 11 months when he finally retired in 1948, aged 70, and had been spent entirely at Mouldsworth as porter and then signalman. The gleaming builders plate shows the frame to have been built at the CLC's Warrington Works in 1894. The track diagram shows the layout until 1943 when the connection to the Helsby branch were lengthened to hold 70 wagon trains.   *M A Birt Collection*

(Above) **Mouldsworth Junction, June 1957:** All country stations had their quiet moments. Porter Eric Cowup and Signalman Herbert Woodward await the next round of business. The rather fine CLC signalbox of 1894 still survives, albeit rebuilt on a brick base, but is no longer a junction since traffic on the West Cheshire branch ceased in the Autumn of 1991.   *N Jones*

Mouldsworth, 3rd August 1958: 'J10/4' No. **65169** arrives with the pick up from Chester, loaded on this occasion with scrap from Northgate for weighing at Mouldsworth. Other traffic at this time included timber from Mickle Trafford and Cuddington, but was not to last much longer. On the left is the site of the terminus of the proposed Tarporley Light Railway of 1904, intended to serve the fairly remote and sparsely populated rural country-side between the CLC and the Chester - Crewe main line.
                                                                                                              N Jones

Barrow for Tarvin

(Right) Barrow for Tarvin, September 1949: 'J10' No. **5184** gets away with the 1410 Manchester - Chester service. The Steven's style signalbox was open by 1883 and closed on 23rd November 1958. The station, known as Tarvin for Barrow until November 1883, closed completely on 1st June 1953.
W A Camwell

(Above-left) Barrow for Tarvin, 12th July 1966: The imposing station bore little relationship to the scattered rural community nearby and probably had much more to do with placating the local landowner Lord Cholmondeley! Thirteen years after closure, the twin pavilioned buildings similar to and contemporary with those on the CLC Liverpool - Manchester main line still retain an air of distinction as the 1500 Manchester - Chester DMU passes by. Remarkably, they still survive today in private ownership.
B Sullivan/T Tomalin

(Above-right) Barrow for Tarvin, c. 1910. This Edwardian view looking towards Mouldsworth shows the charm of Cheshire Lines country stations. The well manicured gardens highlight the pride with which staff went about their work, although the extremely rural location of the station brought about its early demise.
T Booth Collection

Plemstall Crossing, July 1960: '04/7' No. **63600** and a Stanier '8F' double-head a lengthy freight for Dee Marsh whilst the crossing keeper tends his allotment - once a common feature of railway embankments but rarely seen today. Both locomotives are blowing off as they take the slack out of the train and emerge from the dip at the crossing of the River Gowy preparing for the sharp rise at 1 in 75/73 through Mickle Trafford and across the Birkenhead Joint Line towards Chester.
N Jones

Mickle Trafford

Mickle Trafford, 1911: A period scene as an excursion to New Brighton composed of vintage six wheeled stock is signalled away. The external communication cord on the carriage roofs can be seen together with the CLC signalbox and Birkenhead Joint Line in the distance. *J F Ward Collection*

The Beeching way to Manchester Central, via Mickle Trafford

(Above) **Mickle Trafford East, 1949:** Unlike Barrow, Mickle Trafford had to be content with economically constructed wooden buildings of strikingly similar design to those mass produced by the LNWR. The Birkenhead Joint station was immediately north of the signal on the right, and the CLC station became 'Mickle Trafford East' from 5th June 1950, but lack of patronage saw closure to passengers on 12th December 1951. The goods yard on the left, behind the signalbox, once a source of significant timber traffic, closed on 1st July 1963. *A Willis Collection*

(Left) **Mickle Trafford Junction, 1962:** The complex history of the junction is dealt with in the text, but the 1942 connection is prominent in this view of a Chester - Manchester DMU passing the CLC box which was replaced by a modern BR structure from 7th September 1969. The CLC goods shed can be seen behind the train with the Birkenhead Joint Line on the right, together with the brick built Mickle Trafford West box. In the distance the CLC can be seen making the curving climb at 1 in 73 across the Birkenhead Joint which even as late as the mid 'Sixties, involved the provision of a banking engine for heavy freights to Dee Marsh at certain times of day. Mickle Trafford West station was immediately behind the photographer. *A Willis Collection*

The approach to
Chester

(Above) **Chester East Junction, 23rd March 1954.** Trains for Chester Northgate from Mickle Trafford approached the junction and its 15mph speed limit along this straight stretch of line through the Hoole district of the town. The lowered signal indicates a clear run through to the station. The right hand arm of the bracket was for entry into the goods yard, those to left for the Shotton line. The bridge in the foreground carried the line CLC over the Birkenhead line and was numbered 230 on the Altrincham to Chester route. As an intersection bridge, it also carried the number 12 on the Chester Station and Yard line of the GW & LMS Joint Railway. *(Below)* A view of bridge 230 at rail level from the Chester side looking towards Hooton on the Birkenhead route. Lines on the extreme left connected with the Holyhead route adjacent to Chester No. 6 box.   ***Information courtesy J Dixon***

Chester Northgate MPD

Chester Northgate Shed, c. 1938: 'C13' No. **5047** is coming off shed. Opened about 1875, the depot was a subshed of Northwich until 1923. The 1930 allocation was six 'C13s' for Manchester and Wrexham services, five 'N5s' for shunting and goods work, and one 'J63' 0-6-0 tank for shunting at Connahs Quay. Between 1929 and 1941 there was a Sentinel steam railcar for the Hawarden Bridge service. In the 1940s ex GNR 'C12s' were drafted in, together with 'D6' 4-4-0s between 1940 - 43. The shearlegs and stockpiled coal supplies were very much a feature of the large, but rarely very busy shed yard. *B Matthews Collection*

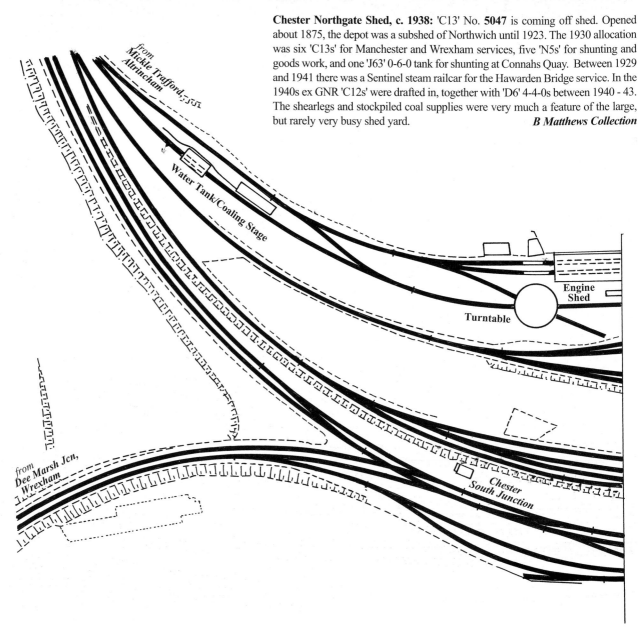

Chester Northgate MPD c. 1955: Remarkably, Great Central tanks could still be seen operating from Chester as late in 1957 on both Wrexham and Manchester services. 'C13' No. **67400** and 'N5' No. **69304** stand outside the shed which, like Northwich, was re-roofed in the early 'Fifties. In BR days the shed also used a variety of loaned and allocated LMS types, including '2P' 4-4-0s and a popular batch of Ivatt class '2' tanks from about 1953 onwards. BR Standard Class '2s' and '4s' were also seen in the period up to dieselisation and closure on 4th January 1960.   *N R Knight*

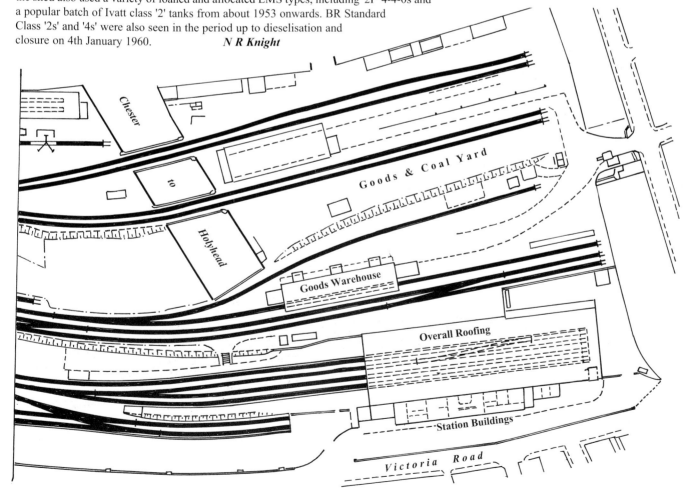

Chester Northgate

(Left) Class C14 4-4-2T No **67449** stands in Chester Northgate (6D) yard on 20th August 1955. The engine was allocated to Wrexham (6E).

(Below) On the same date, with Gorton (39A) allocated K3/2 Class Mogul No **61808** alongside, Class C13 4-4-2T No **67413** of Wrexham (6E) stands at Chester Northgate, attached to a makeshift 'tender' for an 'out and back' freight working where coal would otherwise not be available for the return run.

Brian Morrison

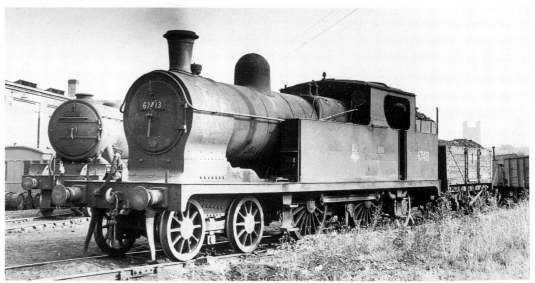

(Below) **Chester South Junction, 10th May 1949:** 'D10' No. **62650** *Prince Henry* leaves with the 1844 to Manchester Central. The box controlled the western arm of the triangular junction with the Dee Marsh line and was opened in August 1889, closing on 6th October 1969. Northgate station and its very substantial station yard are behind the locomotive and the large goods shed can be glimpsed between the engine and signalbox. In the 'Fifties there was also a large Fyffes banana depot served from Garston with onward distribution throughout the area by road. The whole layout was abandoned from 6th October 1969 apart from the route from Mickle Trafford to Dee Marsh.

P M Alexander/Millbrook House

(Above) **Chester Northgate, c. 1961.** Looking north towards the triangular junction with the Mickle Trafford to Dee Marsh line. A Wrexham train is signalled out of Platform 2 and the large station yard and facilities appear as relatively deserted as always. With the station box and signals prominent, the atmosphere is still very much CLC orientated, although modernisation in the form of electric lighting has reached the platforms. ***Stations UK***

Chester Northgate, 20th August 1955. 'Director' **Class D11/1** No. **62661** *Gerard Powys Dewhurst* waits alongside Platform 1 with a train for Manchester Central. ***Brian Morrison***

Chester Northgate, April 1914: The CLC's modest but appealing Chester terminus captured on a quiet Sunday morning. The twin trainsheds and neat buildings with an extensive range of facilities showed clearly that the CLC intended to make an impression in this important regional centre and county town. The left hand trainshed was demolished about 1962, and the whole site is now a leisure centre. *L&GRP - T E Talbot Collection*

Railway Heyday, April 1914: The interior of Chester Northgate provides a distinct impression of discipline, order and prosperity in the halcyon years before the First World War when railways answered virtually all the country's transport needs. The world order is about to be rudely shattered in a few months time, and after the conflagration the pre eminence of railways will be increasingly challenged by road transport. Chester Northgate closed on 6th October 1969 with the Manchester services directed to Chester General, and with no room for a competing service to the direct Wrexham service on the ex GWR main line. *L&GRP - T E Talbot Collection*

Chester Northgate, c. 1930. The elaborately attractive double trainshed was never really quite matched in scale by the surrounding station buildings, and the aspect beyond the bufferstops was always very open. The station was nevertheless perhaps a brave attempt by a relatively small company to match Francis Thompson's magnificent facade at 'the other establishment' in another part of the city. *Stations UK*

Chester Northgate - Platform 1, c. 1954. This interior view of the western trainshed reveals a scene familiar to many travellers in the 'Fifties and early 'Sixties as a train of typically mixed LMS suburban stock awaits departure for Manchester. Bicycle racks and platform barrows front the rather distinctively detailed station buildings boasting a fair range of facilities, and an improvement on the purely wooden structures that were deemed adequate for Manchester Central. *Stations U K*

Chester Northgate - Platform 2, c. 1954. In stark contrast to the views on the previous pages, particularly the 1914 illustration, by the mid 'Fifties the long years of reduced wartime maintenance had taken their toll and on this winter's day the problems of waterproofing large trainsheds are all too evident. Platform facilities by this time had also been significantly reduced. *Stations U K*

(Above) **Chester Northgate, 1954:** 'C13' No. **67430** moves away with an evening local to Hawarden Bridge whilst Fairburn 2-6-4 tank No. **42113** prepares to follow with a Manchester service. Train services on the Wrexham line began in 1893 and were withdrawn on closure of the station on 6th October 1969.

J W T House/C L Caddy Collection

(Right) **Chester Northgate, 29th September 1949.** Class C13 4-4-2T No **67433** (Push & pull fitted), stands alongside Platform 1 with the 4.15pm train for Manchester Central. This really was an 'All Stations' train, and at the same time, taking one hour and forty eight minutes for the 38¾ miles to Manchester.

C A Appleton courtesy J Peden

Chester Northgate, c. 1959. A view from Platform 1 looking towards the station 'throat', Chester South Junction box being located to the right of the locomotive. *Stations U K*

In decline

By 1961, the deteriorating state of the eastern train shed had forced its demolition, together with many of the buildings on Platform 2 - rationalisation which was to befall many other similar structures over the next thirty years. Henceforth, the station exhibited a rather desolate air, although in this 1967 view *(Below)* there are plenty of passengers heading for the Class 108 DMU waiting to leave for Manchester. Complete closure was just two years away. *(Centre-right)* The station entrance; the remaining section of the train shed somewhat exaggerating the skeletal framework.

Lens of Sutton

West Cheshire Branch

Mouldsworth, c. 1936: Signalman William Jones takes the single line token from the Fireman of '4F' No. **4352** coming off the Helsby branch with the 1433 Birkenhead Woodside - Northwich Sundays only service, composed of GWR stock. This service operated from 1934 - 38, originally to Knutsford, and was very popular with the day trippers to Delamere Forest. Despite the use of GWR stock, GW timetables did not advertise these trains going beyond Ince and Elton!
M A Birt Collection

The line from Northwich to Helsby was promoted to give a freight outlet via the Birkenhead Joint Line to the GWR system via Saltney as a useful alternative to the LNWR for traffic to the Midlands and the South, and to reach the Mersey at Birkenhead where the CLC established two goods depots for export traffic. Conversely, the GWR obtained rather indirect access to Liverpool without the conflict implied in its use of LNWR tracks. As the CLC was unable to obtain running powers to Birkenhead, the small exchange yard at West Cheshire Junction came to play a crucial role throughout the CLC era.

Leaving Mouldsworth, the branch turned right and fell at 1 in 680/100/143 along the foot of the Cheshire Ridge through Manley, where the trackbed of the former quarry siding could be seen climbing towards the bridge under the Manley-Mouldsworth road and into the quarry immediately beyond. At Helsby and Alvanley the gradient changed to 1 in 400 up past the site of the goods yard (left) and engine shed (right) to climb over the Warrington-Chester line, before falling at 1 in 70 over a troublesome embankment across open countryside, which delayed the opening to West Cheshire Junction for several months. A short westward curve then led to the isolated West Cheshire Junction on the line from Helsby to Hooton.

Passenger traffic was not expected to be significant, since Helsby with a population of around 700 was given a 'second class station'. There was no interchange point with the Birkenhead Joint Line which also served the village and services were withdrawn immediately once the Mouldsworth-Chester line opened on 1st May 1875. Latterly, just two trains ran from Helsby to Manchester Oxford Road at 0730 and 1630, with return services at 0910 and 1710 from Manchester, together with a Fridays only 1200 Helsby-Northwich train. Manley station never reopened to passengers, but the Helsby facilities hibernated for over fifty years before experiencing a revival. Expansion of the BICC factory close to the station saw the LMS introduce a work people's service to Hooton in October 1936. Five hundred passengers per day were anticipated, and the wartime expansion of the works saw the trains continue unadvertised, into BR days. The 'Girls Train' arrived from Hooton at 0743, 1115SO (ECS), and 1759 SX (ECS), returning at 0755 (ECS), 1125SO and 1800 SX, the stock stabling in West Cheshire yard. By the 'Fifties, the trains were running to Rock Ferry at similar times. Curiously, Helsby and Alvanley was officially 'closed' from 25th February 1944, miraculously 'reopening' on 9th September 1963 when services were advertised before being finally withdrawn on 6th January 1964. But this is not the end of the strange saga of passenger services on this line. By 1934, a Thursdays and Sundays only Birkenhead-Knutsford service operated, which in 1937 was booked to leave Helsby at 1129 and 1522, returning at 1328 and 2036. Powered by a '4F' on Great

Western stock, the trains, which were used mainly by day-trippers to Delamere Forest, were cut back to Sundays only to Northwich by 1937, and did not run after 1939. In the late 'Fifties the branch was sometimes used by DMU excursions from South Manchester to North Wales with reversal at Hooton, as the Mickle Trafford connection was not signalled for propelling movements.

Locomotives stabled at Helsby from the outset, and a fifty foot turntable and engine siding existed just west of the station on the Up side. In 1893, after the CLC finally failed to get running powers to Birkenhead, a two road shed was at last provided. In 1886, two locomotives were sub-shedded from Northwich. '6A' 0-6-0 No. 375 worked the 1850 goods to Ardwick, went to Gorton for coal, working back at 0325 with the crew travelling 98 miles in an eleven hour shift. '23' 0-6-0 No. 137 took the 2000 goods to Manchester Central, coaling at Cornbrook, returning with the 0140 to Helsby. Locomotives were changed at Northwich (for No. 226 another '23'), arrival at West Cheshire Junction being at 0330. The men booked off at 0430 after ten hours and seventy-four miles travelling. Although it was the only CLC shed not involved in the 1926 General Strike, the depot was closed in 1929 with its workings taken over by Northwich and Chester. The final allocation is believed to have been 'J9s' No. 739 Driver W. Thomas, 740 A Haynes, 741 W. Southern, and 'J10s' No. 639 W. Clark, and 675 H. Breeze. The engine siding remained in occasional use until the 'Fifties, but the fifty foot turntable was generally too small by then.

In 1911, Helsby saw eleven Up and ten down freights daily, running to Manchester Central, Trafford Park, Godley, Heaton Mersey and Huskisson via Skelton Junction. There were six connecting services to Birkenhead. In 1937 there were five Up goods to Northwich, one each to Trafford Park and Heaton Mersey, and light engines to Northwich and Chester. On the Down road came three goods from Heaton Mersey, three from Trafford Park, two from Northwich, with light engines from Northwich and Chester. World War Two brought a substantial increase in traffic to the GWR, Birkenhead Docks, and to the rapidly developing chemical plants at Stanlow and Ellesmere Port. Delays were chronic, and the 131 wagon West Cheshire Yard could not be extended. £8700 was therefore spent in doubling the approach at Mouldsworth to accommodate two seventy wagon

trains in each direction before the start of the single line. Auxiliary tablet instruments were needed, worked by manually powered dynamos which called for some dexterity to turn and extract the tablet at the same time!

From early BR days, most trains began to work through to either Saltney or Birkenhead. In 1954, eight Down and six Up services ran, including the 1225 Trafford Park-Croes Newydd, 0415 Warrington CLC-Saltney, 0330 empties Wallerscote to Holywell Junction and the usual Trafford Park and Northwich to Saltney or Birkenhead some of which reversed from West Cheshire Junction to Helsby to gain the route to Chester. By 1961 twelve Down and fourteen Up services reflected the increase in petrol traffic after the opening of the Northwich chord, plus the usual Saltney and Birkenhead trains. Petrol traffic was to sustain the line for the next twenty years, aided by new fertiliser traffic from the UKF plant at Ince. In 1984, some four Up and five Down block workings to Ince or Stanlow used the branch. This traffic declined somewhat in the late 'Eighties but was balanced by export coal and Freightliner workings routed from Crewe to Ellesmere Port and with the prospect of future Channel Tunnel traffic, the line appeared reasonably secure.

Two local sources of freight traffic came from Manley Quarry and the BICC plant at Helsby. The quarry owners provided land for the line in return for a siding taken at significant cost and a 1 in 50 gradient directly into the quarry which opened about 1800 and supplied stone for local building, including the West Cheshire Stations west of Cuddington. The quarry was worked for 80-90 years and must have been a very difficult place to shunt. British Insulated Callendars opened their cable works alongside the goods yard at Helsby in 1916. The factory generated much traffic in World War Two and was served by a daily afternoon trip from Helsby well into the 'Sixties.

Disaster struck in September 1991 when West Cheshire Junction box was seriously damaged by fire. All services from Crewe were diverted, reversing at Warrington to reach Helsby, with the West Cheshire branch 'put out of use' from October 1991 as the cost of signalling repairs could not be justified. Unfortunately, in the 'Nineties, chemical and fertilizer traffic from the Stanlow complex has virtually ceased, and the line remained 'mothballed' for some years before being lifted in 1999.

Manley, c. 1932: The station is seen shortly before the introduction of key token working between Mouldsworth and West Cheshire Junction and the conversion of the signalbox to a ground frame. The station closed to passengers on 1st May 1875 and to goods on 6th March 1961. Between 1869 and about 1900, a steeply graded spur left the yard behind the station to serve Manley Quarry which opened about 1800 to provide stone for various local building projects, including the West Cheshire stations. The station buildings still survive, tastefully restored as a private dwelling.
T Booth Collection

Helsby and Alvanley, 19th July 1963: The original terminus of the West Cheshire Railway opened for goods on 1st September 1869 and to passengers on 22nd June 1870, the goods extension to West Cheshire Junction opening on 14th June 1871. Passenger services ceased on 1st May 1875, but workmen's trains from the Wirral began running for the BICC plant in October 1936. Officially, the station closed again on 25th February 1944, and the workmen's services ran unadvertised for another nineteen years until the station 'reopened' from 9th September 1963 before final withdrawal on 6th January 1964. The siding on the right provided access to the goods yard which closed on 2nd March 1964. Both siding and water tank had disappeared by 1966.

P E Baughan

Helsby and Alvanley, c. 1912: The station staff pose with a Sacre '18' class 0-6-0. A similar locomotive stands on the shed through the bridge to the right. Helsby had an allocation from 1869, but not until 1893 was a two road shed provided after the CLC has failed to secure running powers to Birkenhead. Northwich crews 'on loan' were allowed 1hr 55minutes 'walking time' from Mouldsworth! An engine siding and 50ft turntable survived until the 'Fifties. The signalbox opened in 1883, being replaced by a ground frame in 1932. The goods yard and BICC factory were on the left beyond the bridge. The photograph was rescued from the Northwich shed lobby, where it was displayed for many years.

W Egerton Collection

West Cheshire Junction

West Cheshire Junction, 2nd April 1957: BR Standard 2-6-4 tank No. **80063** comes off the West Cheshire branch with the 1758 Helsby and Alvanley - Rock Ferry "Girls Train". The head shunt for the small exchange yard at West Cheshire Junction is on the right. *N Jones*

West Cheshire Junction, 2nd April 1957: A 'Super D' 0-8-0 heads an eastbound tanks haul past the junction with the CLC. The yard on the left was a key exchange point until the early 'Fifties, with traffic handed over for Birkenhead Docks and the GWR via Saltney. Unfortunately, vandals set fire to the box in September 1991 and the cost of signalling repairs was sufficient to put the Mouldsworth line 'out of use' from 20th October. *N Jones*

The Winsford Branches

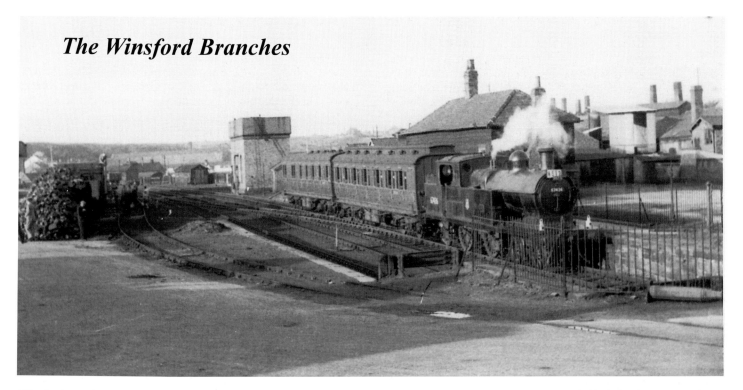

Winsford and Over, 17th October 1953: 'C13' No. **67436,** with an RCTS special, stands in the station, tucked away behind the High Street and surrounded by saltworks and Victorian terraces. The wooden building of very plain, hipped roof construction was part of the original Northwich station, transferred to Winsford "to reduce cost to the lowest possible point" - £5428, indicating that the passenger extension from Falks Junction was very much an afterthought. On the right are the chimneys of Birkenhead Salt Works across the river, whilst the siding in the foreground served Bridge Salt Works which closed in 1928/9, being needed latterly to supply coal to Winsford Gas Works until falling finally out of use about 1961. The line closed from Falks Junction on 1st May 1965, but had seen hardly any use for at least two years previously. *B Hilton*

THE WINSFORD BRANCHES - A CASE OF OVERKILL?

The Winsford salt trade and its associated coal traffic was undoubtedly a great attraction for both the CLC and LNWR, but how this small town of some 10000 souls could support three stations - two of them providing quite indirect services - is another matter. For years the confusingly named termini at Winsford and Over, and Over and Wharton, unfruitfully confronted each other on opposite sides of the Weaver separated by a blanket of salt works smoke. A rapid exit by rail was impossible anyway since the main line station was half an hour's trek from the town centre.

The CLC branch diverged southwards at Winsford Junction ³/₄ mile west of Cuddington, climbing at 1 in 82/127 through forested heathland to Whitegate (3 miles), after which there was a steady fall across embankments and cuttings at 1 in 133/80 past Catscleugh Crossing to Falks Junction (5¹/₄ miles). Here the Winsford extension turned sharp right to follow the Weaver Valley to Winsford and Over (6¹/₄ miles), close to the town centre. The original route terminated in sidings alongside the Meadow Bank road, but was soon extended across the road to Falks works, latterly the site of Victoria Works and the Rock Salt Mine.

As already noted, the CLC passenger service was very much an afterthought, and was suspended twice before being reintroduced by law in 1892. However, a commendable effort was then made to serve the town and in 1911 eight trains left Cuddington at 0640, 0805, 0915, 1225, 1415, 1615, 1725, 1832 and 2005, with return workings at 0720, 0840, 1045, 1300, 1450, 1755, 1900 and 2055. Good connections allowed the eleven mile journey to Northwich to be made in ³/₄ hour by most services.

Road competition and the depression of the 'Twenties saw receipts halved from £1706 in 1921 to £809 in 1930. The Sentinel steam railcar introduced in 1929 cut running costs by two thirds, but savings of £3275 per year were still achieved by withdrawal of the passenger trains from 1st January 1931. As little as £159 per annum was being generated by purely local traffic. The 1874 withdrawal had been due to lack of patronage, and that in 1888 to Board of Trade objections to 'mixed' trains and the state of the signalling and interlocking. Lord Delamere had provided land for the extension to Winsford on condition that a passenger service was maintained, and in 1891 Winsford Council obtained an order from the Railway Commissioners that "all reasonable facilities should be provided for forwarding and delivering passenger traffic" which secured the reintroduction of services. In 1931 the Council tried a further approach to the Commissioners, but the CLC had arranged for parcels to go by freight train, and for the extension of the Northwich bus service to Northwich station with additional busses from Cuddington to Winsford. The Commission considered that 'reasonable' arrangements had indeed been made and there was no third reinstatement of the train service.

Until 1929, trains ran to Cuddington (except for two through to Northwich on Saturdays), worked by Northwich engines sub shedded at Winsford. The wooden shed with 45 foot turntable opened in June 1870 being enlarged to two roads for the 1892 reinstatement of passenger services. In 1886, class '23' 0-6-0 No. 50 was at Winsford, making four trips to Cuddington in a working day from 0700 to 1830 in which it covered 56 miles, 36 of them on shunting duties which must have been considerable! After 1892 the depot had two locomotives, a Sacre '9B'/E' 0-6-0 for freight and sometimes a '12A' 2-4-0 for passengers. Later, Northwich had 'F1' 2-4-2 tanks Nos. 583, 600 and 726, No. 600 being a regular on Winsford services until 1929, after which both passenger and freight services were reorganised to be worked from Northwich and Winsford shed closed, being demolished soon afterwards.

Freight services were dominated by salt and coal, some 29,000 tons of the former being despatched in 1910, about half the LNWR total and barely a tenth of that handled on the Weaver. In 1911, four trains ran at 0630, 1110, 1515 and 1935 from Winsford, returning at 0740, 1244 and 1637 from Cuddington and 1620 from Northwich. There was a 1000 conditional path for coal empties to Haydock worked by a Northwich locomotive via Skelton Junction, whilst salt specials ran to Grimsby, lodging turns from Winsford men on which they were often away for 3 - 4 days! By 1937, three daily trips ran from Northwich, reduced to a morning and afternoon working in early BR days. The 'J10s' remained on the job until the mid 'Fifties when '4Fs' took over, followed by Ivatt and BR standard 2-6-0s on what were quite heavy trains, the afternoon battle on Whitegate bank being of much more interest to your author than school games!

At Winsford there were about eight saltworks to be served on the west bank of the Weaver, the Vacuum Plant of 1906 and the Rock Salt Mine developed from 1928 after the Northwich mines flooded, providing the basic traffic in latter years. Most of the salt works on the Winsford extension had closed by the late 'Fifties and Winsford and Over closed to goods in September 1958 when facilities were concentrated on Over and Wharton. Coal was occasionally delivered over the weed covered tracks to Hamlett's Salt Works which closed in 1961, the line from Falks Junction

being 'put out of use' from 1st May 1965. It was finally visited at Wades Crossing in 1968 when a road was being built to the new sewage plant and a Class '40' was sent to 'protect' the proceedings!

In the harsh winters of the mid 'Sixties, rock salt traffic built up steadily, but a decision was taken to transport this by road to Over and Wharton. The number of lorry loads was controversial, but the main flow was to Scotland and the North and it made sense to distribute this via the main line. Rail traffic on the CLC branch ceased from 13th March 1967, official closure following from 11th February 1968. Four years later, much of the route became a country footpath, the 'Whitegate Way'.

The origin of the LNWR branch to Over and Wharton can be traced to the fascinating system of mineral branches built after 1840 to link the Grand Junction Railway with the Salt Works on Wharton Common. By 1870, there were four branches between Verdin Sidings and Kays Crossing (Winsford Junction), the most southerly leading to the Wharton Railway and River Works. From this line, a south facing spur led under Wharton Road to Lycett's Coal Wharf, on the west side of, but not connected to, the main line.The indications are that between 1840-70 there was a direct, facing connection from the main line to the Wharton salt works along the line of 'Lycetts Railway', but definite proof is lacking and the coal wharf had been abandoned by 1910. In 1880, the LNWR opened a branch from Kays Crossing to R.Evans and Co's Liverpool Works, together with the Brine Branch to Verdin's Birkenhead Works. This involved using the first part of the Railway and River Works branch and cutting across the spur to Lycett's Wharf. Two years later, the LNWR converted the Liverpool Works line into a double track, 1mile 22yard branch to its new station at Over and Wharton. Curving sharply westwards at Winsford Junction, the line soon reached Brine Branch Box (Leycette Ground Frame after 1925). Here, the Lycett's Wharf

Over and Wharton, 16th June 1947: The last day of passenger services finds 0-6-2 tank No. **6906** waiting to leave with the last train, empty stock to Warrington - this was the one train of the day not worked by the Wharton based motor set. Services had previously been suspended as a wartime economy between January 1917 and July 1920. After the Second World War competition from the North Western Road Car Co. was severe and there was little future for the six or so unevenly timed and inconvenient services on the branch.

W A Camwell

Winsford from the air, c. 1935: The constricted Weaver Valley, packed with salt works before the Second World War. Over and Wharton LNWR station is just off the picture, bottom right, whilst the CLC branch from Falks Junction (**1**) snakes along the valley to Winsford and Over signalbox (**2**). In the centre, Simpson, Davies & Sons Wharton Meadow Works (**3**) is reached by a frail bridge. To the south of Wades Crossing (**4**) is Wood End Works and Deakin's Over Works Siding (**5**) the scene of the 1888 accident. Meadow Bank Crossing (**6**) is on the branch to Victoria, Coronation and Falks Works (later the Meadow Bank Rock Salt Mine). The Brine Branch (**7**) descends through the river terrace to R Evan's Uploont Works (**8**) and Verdin's Birkenhead Works (**9**) below Over and Wharton station. Kay's Cheshire Amalgamated Works (**10**) and Stubbs Littlemeadow Works by the river are served by branch and wagon hoist from Winsford Junction. The remains of Dutch Salt Works, closed by the 'Thirties, are in the foreground (**11**).

Cheshire County Library

spur diverged left, with the branch to the Railway and River Works and the Brine Branch diverging right, the latter running parallel for a quarter of a mile before descending for 981 yards through the river terrace to the Weaverside Birkenhead Works. The new branch featured several sturdy blue brick bridges replacing flat crossings, which together with those on the Lycett branch and main line saw the area known as 'Wharton Bridges' to several generations of Winsfordians. The line then continued mostly in cutting, past the Brine Branch divergance, until a left hand curve with Liverpool Works to the west, led to the neat terminus overlooking the Weaver Valley and town centre.

Alas, the passenger service was always meagre, up to a maximum of six trains per day to Runcorn or South Lancashire towns, and after 1911, the service was usually worked by a Warrington 2-4-2 tank and motor set sub shedded at Wharton. Trains were suspended as a wartime economy from 1st January 1917 until 12th July 1920. On reopening, the line was converted to single line working, with the old up road becoming a long siding. In 1919 departures were at 0720 to Newton le Willows, 1030 to Hartford (Warrington SO), 1428 to Hartford (St. Helens WSO), and 1635 to Acton Bridge. Arrivals were at 1017 from Hartford, 1144 from Hartford (SX), 1319 from Newton le Willows (SO), 1455 from Hartford (WSX), 1549 from St. Helens WSO), and 1837

from Earlestown, hardly a frequent or uniform provision! There was never a Sunday service in either of the Winsford branches.

By 1938, the service provided was still minimal, although it probably saved the LMS stopping some semi-fasts at Preston Brook or Moore. Trains left at 0623 to Runcorn, 0725 and 1025 to Warrington(Wigan SO), 1425(SO) and 1625 to Acton Bridge. Arrivals were 0716ECS from Runcorn, 0903 and 1336(SO) from Acton Bridge, 1553 (1600SO) from Warrington, 1833(SX) from St. Helens and 1905(SO) from Warrington. The final service in 1947 saw departures at 0617 for Acton Bridge, 0725 to Warrington, 1130(SO) and 1620 to Acton Bridge, with arrivals at 0702 from Hartford, 0922 from Warrington, 1313(SO) from Acton Bridge, 1756 from Acton Bridge (not a motor set) and 1857 from Warrington, very few of these services enjoying good connections. The branch engine was double shifted by two crews based at Over and Wharton, who sometimes worked evening excursions to Northwich or Warrington in place of the regular 2227(SO) from Warrington which ran until the 1917 cuts.

Latterly the trains were mostly used by workers and children from Acton Bridge going to school in Winsford who were easily accommodated by the North Western Road Car Co. when the LMS withdrew the service 'as a coal economy measure' from 16th June 1947.

Cuddington

Cuddington, c. 1930: Sentinel railcar No. **602** is at the Down platform with a Winsford service. The somewhat breathless railcar could delay Up services if turned out first at Winsford Junction to the irritation of the Cuddington clientele of Manchester cotton merchants. Confronted by one irate commuter, Porter 'Scroper' Dunn had the answer in springing to attention, saluting in the best military manner and declaring that "We are waiting for the Sentinel Sir".

L&GRP, courtesy NRM

Salt and coal dominated the freight traffic, some 57,000 tons of white salt moving from LNWR outlets in 1910. In 1916 the daily road trip from Warrington arrived at 1350 having shunted the Brine Branch, and returned at 1415. By 1939, the branch also had a trip from Crewe (Trip 35) which arrived in the early afternoon, worked both branches and returned at 1730. By 1960 the Warrington train was MWFO, arriving about 1230 and leaving around 1500. Some down freights also detached goods for Winsford at the Junction. During World War Two the yard here was often busy shunting Winsford traffic which had arrived in rough cuts to relieve pressure on Basford Hall. Coal traffic was significant until about 1955 and general goods were handled after about 1925 when Winsford Goods Yard closed, similar traffic being transferred from the CLC branch in 1958. The Crewe trip (Target 22) still ran in 1961, but ceased soon afterwards. It was booked to arrive at 0820 but often ran much later, returning light engine at 1440, '3F' and '4F' 0-6-0s being the usual power. Domestic coal kept the Warrington trip going until closure to goods in September 1968, with the Brine Branch still operational until 1966/67 for traffic to Colin Stewart's works. In former years, Salt Union locomotives travelled between Birkenhead and Uploont works and their shed on the former Liverpool Works site, using the Brine Branch

and the section between Brine Branch Junction and Over and Wharton. In 1948 the engine came off shed at 0934, returning at 1243, leaving at 1343 before returning finally at 1647. Ten years earlier, similar movements had been common throughout the branch and along the goods siding linking the various salt works as far as Verdin Sidings on the main line.

Rock salt traffic increased dramatically in the mid 'Sixties, and in 1966 110,000 tons were moved from Over and Wharton, three trains of 5 - 600 tons leaving nightly for Scottish destinations in the winter of 1966/67. In March 1967 the CLC branch closed and all rail traffic was concentrated on the LNW branch. A Northwich '8F' was booked to shunt the branch throughout the day making up trains for direct despatch on the main line, and working two trips to Northwich for other destinations. Traffic flourished throughout the 'Seventies when the yard at Over and Wharton was simplified and all buildings demolished to facilitate loading operations. Traffic was so heavy that the branch had to be closed for relaying from 3rd October 1982, reopening in June 1983. Unfortunately climatic factors have since intervened and traffic declined to perhaps only four or five trains in the winter of 1989 - 90. The branch then became easy prey to a local housing and road development scheme and was lifted in the spring of 1991.

Winsford Junction, CLC, 12th April 1968: The sixteen lever box, in use by 1883 and opened as required, was located on the fringe of Delamere Forest and is seen two months after the Winsford branch officially closed, traffic having ceased from 13th March 1967. Curiously, the original block section was from Falks Junction to Cuddington, possibly to avoid stopping trains at the foot of the steep rise from Winsford Junction. The signalman here needed a strong constitution: he had a mile to walk from Cuddington station and was presented with a dead fox accompanying the single line staff on one occasion! *H B Priestley*

Whitegate, September 1958: Someone has mastered the shy steaming '4F' No. **44155** as she climbs through Whitegate with T53 the afternoon return trip to Northwich. ICI bulk salt 'Presflo' wagons from the Winsford vacuum plant form the head of the train which is heading towards Delamere Forest from which many unofficial 'orders' for Christmas trees were taken during the festive season! *J I C Boyd*

The Whitegate Way

(Centre) **Whitegate, c. 1925:** A picture taken from the signalbox of this comprehensively signalled wayside station where there was clearly time to produce immaculate station gardens! The signal box and loop were installed in 1891 at the peak of salt traffic, but the box was replaced by ground frames from 6th July 1947. Goods traffic - mainly coal and potatoes survived precariously until 4th November 1963 after closure to passengers on 1st January 1931. The sidings were often used for staging loads on the stiff 1 in 80 climb from Falks Junction on which a 'J10' was allowed 26 of mineral or 40 empties. The ground frames closed on 19th July 1964.

L A Earle Collection

(Lower) **Whitegate, c. 1930:** For the last eighteen months, passenger services were operated by the brand new Sentinel steam railcar No. **602,** this and three sister vehicles being the only motive power actually owned by the CLC. The railcar reduced expenses by £1300 p.a., but to no avail since passenger numbers fell by 32% between 1924 and 1930 and a loss of £4154 was still recorded.

T Booth Collection

(Above) **Meadow Bank, 21st February 1959:** No. **44155** brings a train out of Victoria Works and the Rock Salt Mine. The steam sanders are on for the steep rise across the road and up to Falks Junction which made this a very difficult place to get out of. On the right is the River Weaver with the West Coast Main Line on the horizon, just beyond the opposite river bank. *J I C Boyd*

(Right) **Victoria Works, Winsford, 1951:** Veteran Fletcher Jennings 0-4-0 tank *Victoria* of 1882 is typical of the great variety of industrial locomotives in the Winsford area. The engine worked at the Salt Union's West Works, having moved from the Parkside Mining Co., Frizington, Cumbria, and was scrapped in 1953. She is pictured alongside one of the clinker walls which were once a characteristic of the district, the clinkers being a product of coal burning in the open pan method of salt production.. *F Jones*

(Below) **Baker's Lane Crossing, 17th October 1953:** 'C13' No. **67436** propels an RCTS special composed of an LNER push and pull set past the site of Wood End Works towards Wades Crossing and Falks Junction. To the right, Over Works provides a still characteristic industrial background to a scene that was to change completely over the next ten years. Along with other local railways, the line hereabouts suffered badly from brine subsidence and in 1916 was nearly temporarily truncated at this point. After 1892 the line on the right was a through goods siding from Falks Junction to Winsford, accessing the West Bank salt works. By 1953, only Over Works and Meadow Workshops remained, the latter providing occasional traffic until about 1964/65. *N Fields*

Over and Wharton Shed, 16th June 1947: Coal tank No. **6906** takes water having worked in from Warrington, whilst the motor tank sub shedded from Warrington resides in the shed which closed on 27th August that year. The small 18 lever LNW signal box was then the domain of Signalmen Joe Cross and Tom Sanbach but closed when electric token working gave way to One Engine in Steam in November 1952. The track through the gate led to Liverpool Salt Works closed in the 'Thirties, but was still used for coal to the nearby Birkenhead Works. As late as 1950, Salt Union locomotives regularly used the branch to transfer between works and to reach the S.U. shed on the Liverpool Works site.
W A Camwell

(Centre) **Nat Lane Bridge, March 1959:** The double track branch to Over and Wharton reverted to single line working in 1920 when the former up line became a long siding which was used in 1959 to store LNW 0-8-0s and Tilbury tanks awaiting scrapping. The Brine Branch, having already diverged from the running line, descends through the river terrace to the salt works alongside the Weaver. It remained open until about 1967 for occasional traffic to Colin Stewart's works, salt traffic having ceased some ten years earlier. Over and Wharton closed to goods on 10th June 1968, but rock salt kept the line open until the mild winters of recent years all but killed the traffic and the branch was lifted in March 1991. *A W Martin*

(Lower) **Brine Branch Junction, 6th July 1964:** By LMS days the Wharton branch had two pick ups, one from Crewe, the other from Warrington which often conveyed sludge tenders from the Moore softening plant to Ince Moss Tip. The '3F' hauled Crewe service ceased about 1961, but the Warrington train continued with '4F' power although 'Jubilees' and even a 'Britannia', 'Geoffrey Chaucer', were not unknown! Here, '8F' No. **48558** nears Winsford Junction with the return trip to Warrington. The bridge in the background was the site of Brine Branch box of 1882 - 1920. The right hand archway led to Wharton Railway and River Works of c. 1874 - 1956. To the left of the brake van is the junction for Lycett's coal wharf, closed by 1910. Today, the whole site has disappeared under a new housing development. *A Wilkinson*

The Middlewich Branch

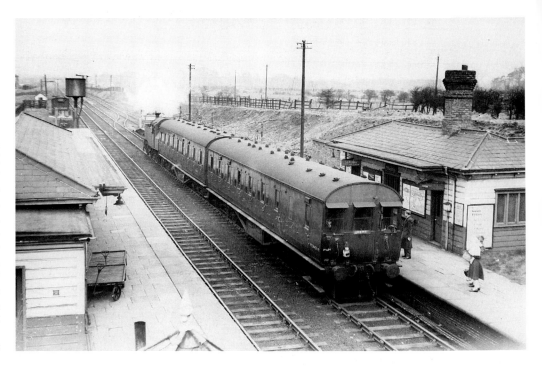

'Thomas, Annie and Clarabel', 14th March 1959: No. 41229 and her two motor coaches M24431M and M15685M call at Middlewich with the 1330 SO Northwich - Crewe. The motor trains running beyond Northwich, together with the Crewe - Liverpool and Warrington services had disappeared in 1941, and after 1931 it was no longer possible to travel from London to Middlewich on the through coach to Manchester Oxford Road. Only four basic services between Crewe and Northwich remained, and No.41212 was to work the last 'Dodger' on 2nd January 1960.
T Lewis courtesy R W Hinton

This relatively unknown branch provided the LNWR's access to the Cheshire Saltfield and until the late 'Sixties tapped significant salt and chemical traffic from both Middlewich and Northwich. With the opening of the Northwich Chord line in 1957, the line gave an invaluable freight bypass for Crewe, and was useful for passenger diversions from the Crewe - Manchester, West Coast, and after 1969, Holyhead main lines. Local traffic was always limited, although some useful trains ran to Lancashire destinations before 1941. After the war, the limited local service suffered badly from bus competition and ceased at the end of 1959. The line's busiest period came late-in the mid 'Sixties - but the closure of the West Cheshire Branch has seriously threatened the line's future and it remains essentially 'mothballed' at present.

From Sandbach, double track leads northwards for ³/4 mile to the divergence on the Down side of the siding to Hayes Chemicals (Formerly Murgatroyds Salt and Chemical Company, established 1949). Single track then descends at 1in 132/152 past the down siding at 1¹/4 miles to British Salt Limited. Until 1979 this works was served by a parallel salt siding from Middlewich, which from 1918 had served the nearby works of Messrs Verdin Cooke & Co. and H W Morris Ltd (later Cerebos Salt Ltd), replacing direct connections from the running line established in 1903. The descent continues at 1 in 1088/168/157 past the Down side site of the General Electrolytic Parent Company's Works of 1899-1928. Immediately on the up side is the site of Cledford Bridge Halt, 2¹/2 miles. The ensuing mile long fall at 1 in 132 is past the down side sites of Brunner Mond's Mid Cheshire Works of 1898-1962, Murgatroyds (1899-1966), Amans, Simpsons, and Seddons salt works (1891-1968), all closely bunched together, with open views across pleasant country to Mow Cop on the up side. Immediately before Middlewich, again on the down side, is the site of the Mid Cheshire Alkali Company's works of 1888-1915, the cause of much disruption until the construction of the salt siding from 1898 onwards.

Middlewich, 3¹/2 miles, had typical LNWR wooden, hipped roofed buildings, those on the Downside surviving in private ownership until the early 'Eighties. The station platforms remain, periodically prompting local calls for reopening. The substantial yard once accommodated extensive wagon storage, at least four coal merchants, and served a wide agricultural hinterland in addition to salt and chemicals. Closure to goods came in November 1967 and since 1970 the yard has been in the hands of a bus contractor. The sixteen lever, LNWR type 4 signalbox of 1892 in which your author spent many happy hours, disappeared in March 1980, replaced by the new powerbox at Hartford. The crossover at the north end of the yard was relocated at the extremity of the headshunt in 1975 to create a long crossing loop, involving the use of auxiliary tablet apparatus. Previously, only 30 wagons could be accommodated, and much setting back into the salt siding was necessary to cross trains. Block working was with train staffs until 1956/7, when miniature tokens were substituted. Middlewich - Sandbach became track circuit block from 1960.

From Middlewich the line rises at 1 in 462, crossing the River Dane on a fine single arched viaduct, and climbs at 1 in 151 above the surrounding fields to Croxton underbridge. A fall at 1 in 132 leads to the crossing of the Trent and Mersey Canal at Whatcroft, and the line is surrounded by salt subsidence 'flashes' on either side of Billinge Green Halt, 7 miles. A descent at 1 in 120 leads to Northwich, with the bypass bridge marking the site on the Up side of Gadbrook Ammunition Siding, opened in 1916 and closed by 1920, but not before it had stored brand new surplus 'WD' '04' 2-8-0s at the end of hostilities. A fine view to the west across the Dane Valley to the West Cheshire's Northwich Viaduct marks the approach to the Northwich triangle, past the former Sandbach Junction and into the down island platform with the actual junction with the CLC now located east of the station.

At first, all passenger trains ran to Crewe because of B.O.T. objections to the lack of a turntable at Sandbach. After 1888, an island platform was provided and until about 1950, some services turned round there. Edwardian times found the branch train affectionately known as the 'Dodger', and in January 1911 motor trains began between Nantwich and Northwich with new motor halts' at Newcastle Crossing, Gresty, and Cledford Bridge close to the Middlewich salt plants. Billinge Green opened a little

Northwich, 22 June 1964. A rail level view towards Chester with Sandbach Junction box just visible beyond the bridge abutment. ***BR-LMR***

later in totally rural countryside near Northwich. Although the Nantwich service did the not survive the First World War, some motor trains continued from Northwich to Acton Bridge, thence to Warrington or Earlestown. Other trains ran between Crewe, Warrington and Liverpool, reversing at Northwich, their locomotives using the CLC turntable. From 1885 to 1931 there was a Manchester Oxford Road - Euston through coach working over the CLC. Immediately before the Second World War there were eight motor trains each way, Liverpool and Warrington - Crewe evening services, two Crewe/Sandbach - Warrington trains, and a summer Saturday Sandbach - Blackpool with a return evening service from Warrington. Services were withdrawn beyond Northwich on 30th June 1941, and from 2nd March 1942 Cledford Bridge and Billinge Green Halts closed. By 1948, the service was down to morning and evening trips with a Saturday lunchtime Sandbach - Northwich working, although the 22.15 SO Northwich - Crewe had survived into 1947. In BR days all trains ran from Crewe, but the service remained just as sparse and faced competition from much more frequent and convenient buses. No. 41212 performed the last rites with the 'Dodger' on the evening of Saturday 2nd January 1960 - a very traumatic occasion for one twelve year old who witnessed the event.

The branch was quite frequently used for main line diversions. From 1957 to 1960 several Manchester expresses including the 'Pines Express' were routed daily via Middlewich. West Coast diversions saw 'Duchess' pacifics proceeding quietly across the Cheshire meadows with the 'Royal Scot' and other prestigious services; later, run down 'Britannias' tackled the climb out of Middlewich with bleary eyed rugby supporters returning to South Wales after Murrayfield Internationals. Some of the last regular traffic on the line between January and May 1992 saw the Sunday 0750 Euston - Holyhead HST and several Chester -

Crewe workings booked this way. The last known passenger use of Middlewich station was on Sunday 21st March 1965 when Crewe - Liverpool locals called in lieu of their usual Winsford stop, and particularly in recent years, the line has often provided overnight stabling for the Royal Train.

Freight services were initially dominated by coal and salt, several 'salt expresses' running daily from Basford Hall to Northwich and Middlewich. Coal was tripped from Lawton Junction to Sandbach for onward despatch by the LNWR, but by 1899 there were some North Staffordshire Railway through workings to Middlewich and Northwich, which continued to the Grouping with a break in 1912/13. The LNWR had through workings to the Potteries via the North Stafford branch, and until the 'Fifties, limestone for Middlewich came from Buxton via Stockport. The Middlewich salt and chemical plants developed rapidly in the eighteen-nineties and a pilot locomotive became necessary. Common salt production reached a peak in 1918 when 383,000 tons was moved from Middlewich. In 1937 there were four North Stafford - Northwich return coal workings, Chatterley - Middlewich coal, two Crewe - Northwich services, the morning train serving Middlewich, and the daily caustic soda train from Middlewich to Crosfields at Warrington. The Crewe South '4F' on the Pilot was treble shifted by Crewe men permanently stationed at Middlewich. The engine arrived light from Northwich having worked the 0530 parcels from Crewe, and then shunted all day in the hands of the early and late turn men. The night shift took the evening transfers to Basford Hall and carried out engine duties at Crewe South before returning on the parcels. From 1950, the job passed to Northwich and superior power in the form of a 'Pom Pom' (J11) 0-6-0. Alas, it was not long before '4Fs' were allocated to Northwich and the shy steaming No. 44155 became the 'regular' at Middlewich. The station was now served by its own afternoon trip from Crewe, usually worked by a '4F' or 'Super D', but also by the prototype class '20' diesels D8000/1 in 1957/8. This hefty train ceased with the closure of the ICI works

Northwich, 22nd June 1964. Another view towards Chester, this time from the Up platform along the main line, the Middlewich branch swinging off to the left.

Northwich, 29th April 1948: From 1911 to 1942 the area bustled with LNWR motor trains powered by Webb 2-4-2 tanks plying between Nantwich, Crewe and Sandbach to Acton Bridge, Ditton Junction and Earlestown, together with the Over and Wharton branch. The Middlewich train - the 'Dodger' - is headed by No. **6681** at Northwich, about to leave for Crewe at 0823. The basic service was soon down to only four daily return trips and Crewe North's last Webb tank No 46680 disappeared in 1953, the service being monopolised from October 1948 by Ivatt tank No. 41229 assisted by numerous ex-works sisters, Stanier 0-4-4 tank No 41901 in 1957/8, and No's 41212 and 41220 from 1958 until the service was withdrawn in 1960.

W A Camwell

in 1962, which also saw the demise of the Pilot, yard staff and the daily return limestone workings to Tunstead. By 1960 most of the salt works had ceased to use rail distribution and the distinctive bauxite vans of Seddons and the yellow, gable roofed Cerebos vans were no more. The daily coal train from Chatterley had ceased by 1964, but the opening of the new British Salt works close to the Cerebos site in 1966 provided useful rail consignments and still does so.

The ten years from 1957 to 1967 were very busy. Regular passenger diversions were accommodated alongside increasing freight flows between the Potteries, East Midlands, Stanlow and Shotwick using the West Cheshire, Middlewich and North Stafford branches to avoid Crewe. Delays could be severe for west bound traffic for the Northwich Chord meeting two or three services in the opposite direction. Some twenty Up and thirty Down trains were booked daily, mostly class 7 services. The main flows were coal and empties from the Potteries to Northwich, Shotwick and Runcorn, tank trains from Stanlow to the Midlands and Potteries, and sand from Oakamoor to Warrington. Monument Lane and Northampton to Northwich vans, Edge Hill - Nottingham and Warrington - Stoke advertised services used the line in both directions. Two Northwich - Crewe transfer freights and the early morning and evening Crewe - Manchester and evening Northwich - Crewe parcels completed the picture. There were times when the Middlewich signalman could be very busy, shunting and staging trains and pacifying marooned traincrews with invitations to visit the 'Boars Head'!

After 1971 when the North Stafford branch closed, it was no longer possible to avoid Crewe, but the Middlewich line remained quite busy into the 'Seventies. There was some decline in petrol traffic and the transfers to Crewe ceased with the run down of Basford Hall yard. The end of steelmaking at Shotwick in 1982 dealt a severe blow to the coal traffic, and with ICI often burning oil, there was no coal traffic for a time in the 'Eighties although some Silverdale - Northwich trains have run since. In 1985, seven down and six up trains were booked - not all of them daily, mainly involving fertiliser from the Shellstar plant at Ince,

and a couple of block tanks from Stanlow. A twice weekly trip ran to Hayes Chemicals and British Salt, but new Freightliner and export coal traffic was developing, routed from Crewe to Ellesmere Port and the future seemed fairly secure.

The line has always seen a wide variety of motive power. In LNWR days anything from 2-4-0's to 'Prince of Wales' 4-6-0's could be seen on the Liverpool and Warrington services, with the usual variety of 0-6-0's and 0-8-0's on goods. In LMS days 'Claughtons' sometimes appeared, including the last survivor No 6004 which was at Edge Hill in the late 'Thirties. The 'Dodger' was the preserve of motor fitted Webb 2-4-2 tanks, Crewe North usually having three supplemented by 'ex works' sisters. The resident in 1944 were No 6605, 6711 and 6742, the last being No 46680 withdrawn early in 1953. Latterly the 'branch engine' was Ivatt class '2' No 41229. Delivered new to Crewe North in October 1948, she was constantly on the branch passenger and parcels workings until transferred to Kingmoor in August 1965. Back up came from No 41320 until 1954, and 0-4-4 No 41901 had a spell in 1957 before Nos 41212 and 41220 arrived in 1958 and stayed until 1965. From 1957, practically the whole range of LMS passenger power could be seen, although class '8P' 4-6-2's were not allowed between Middlewich and Northwich until 1958. Freight trains were largely in the hands of '4F's', 'Super D's', 'Crab' and Stanier 2-6-0's, 'Black Fires' and '8F's', with several Birkenhead '9F' turns in the mid 'Sixties. 'Salt Expresses' could produce all sorts of 'ex works' surprises, including 'Evening Star' on the 2030 Crewe - Northwich on one autumn evening in 1963. Diesels began to appear regularly in 1965, when class '40's' took over some of the heavier petrol workings. They' also took the one coach Crewe-Northwich parcels as a fill in turn! Class '25's' appeared on the Trentham-Shotwick coal hauls from 1967, and class '47's' had infiltrated on some trains. The '47's' have dominated most of the traffic in recent years, although Crewe based '31's' appeared on Freightliner turns with class '37's' on export coal traffic, and class '20's' on other coal trains. More sedate power included the nocturnal activities of Crewe South diesel shunters proceeding from Northwich for refuelling, and there were often contretemps in transferring ICI's Borrows Well tanks - well known for 'breathlessness' and hot boxes - between Middlewich and Northwich without failing in section or running out of water!

The closure of the West Cheshire branch in September 1991 deprived the Middlewich line of all regular traffic except the twice weekly trip from Runcorn to Hayes Chemicals and British Salt via Sandbach. The line was retained for main line diversions in the Spring of 1992, but was closed between the British Salt Siding and Northwich from May 11th. The line, officially 'moth-balled', although used for West Coast freight diversions in 1993, and since has been host to several railtours and the Royal Train.

Fortunately, most of the track and signalling has been renewed in the last twenty years and during the 'Nineties the line continued to be used for main line diversions, including the ICI Hoppers diverted via Stockport and Sandbach on occasion. Hayes Chemicals and British Salt at Middlewich continue to be served by a tripworking from Warrington, now via the Northwich Chord, but interestingly the branch has appeared in Railtrack's ten year Development Plan as part of a westward approach to Manchester Airport via the CLC. The two remaining platforms at Middlewich could have a future after all!

Northwich, c. 1963. The upper and centre views on this page show the Middlewich branch as it leaves the town for open country, firstly beneath footbridge No. 31, a 'standard' LNWR structure, and secondly under a less conventional type of lattice bridge at the point where the branch allowed acces to and from the Northwich west to south curve. **BR-LMR**

(Below) **Billinge Green, 23rd April 1966**: Horwich 'Crab' 2-6-0 No. **42727** heads the RCTS 'St George Railtour'. North of the bridge in the background is the Northwich bypass bridge where Brunner Mond & Co's Gadbrook Explosives Siding of 1916 branched eastwards, one of several World War I munitions installations in the area, it had closed by 1920. To the right is one of the subsidence 'flashes' which border the line hereabouts.

M Mensing

Dane Viaduct, Middlewich, 29th April 1967: Class '9' 2-10-0 No. 92063 crosses the viaduct north of Middlewich with the RCTS 'Wrexham, Mold and Connah's Quay Railtour'. *A Wilkinson*

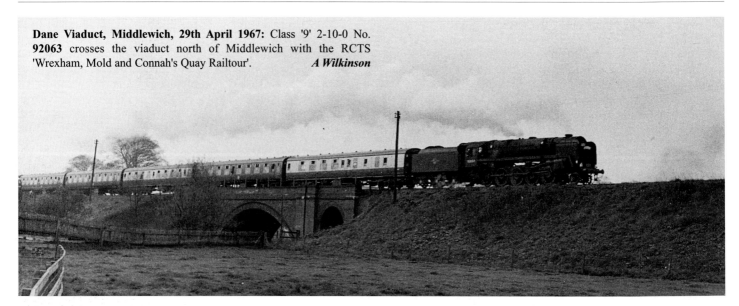

(Centre) **Ravenscroft, October 1964:** The 'branch engine' Ivatt Class '2' tank No **41229** leaves Middlewich with 3H27 1824 Crewe - Manchester Central parcels. New to Crewe North in 1948, she was constantly at work on the branch until transferred to Kingmoor in 1965, being withdrawn in 1966, a mere 18 years old. 3H04 the 0456 Crewe - Manchester parcels served Middlewich from 0515 - 20 until November 1967. The Crewe tanks worked these trains to Northwich, together with 3K19 1924 Northwich - Crewe parcels, which before 1960 attached to the 1850 Northwich - Crewe motor set. After Crewe North closed in May 1965, English Electric Type '4s' were often used, with '8Fs' beyond Northwich. *A Wilkinson*

(Left) **Croxton, c1960:** After 1958, LMS '8Ps' were allowed between Middlewich and Northwich and the 'Duchesses' provided many a Sunday spectacle, making their way sedately across the Cheshire meadows. No. **46247** *City of Liverpool* tops the climb out of Middlewich with the down 'Royal Scot' from Euston to Glasgow. *H Hodgkinson*

Whatcroft, April 1956: Just before the busiest period on the branch with expanding freight traffic from the Wirral and regular passenger diversions from the West Coast Main Line and Manchester routes. Rebuilt 'Royal Scot' No. **46143** *The South Staffordshire Regiment* heads a diverted Euston - Manchester express across the Trent and Mersey canal. *T K Widd*

Through the Cheshire Countryside

(Centre) **Billinge Green, 29th June 1964:** Fresh from overhaul at Crewe, '8F' No **48258** bustles past the site of the halt with the 1806 Stanlow - Colwick tanks. Working to Stoke, Northwich men occasionally got this 500 ton train over the 5.5 miles to Middlewich in as little as eight minutes! The Crewe South '8F' worked to Birkenhead, then to Colwick. A fill-in turn to Wychnor Sidings followed before returning on the next day's Colwick - Stanlow tanks. The halt, opened by the LNWR about 1911 in very rural territory, closed as a wartime economy on 2nd March 1942.
A Wilkinson

(Lower) **Middlewich, 5th February 1966.** The 'Locomotive Club of Great Britain' operated two separate 'Pull and Push Farewell' Railtours on the 5th and 12th February respectively. Starting from Earlestown, the two-coach train was propelled on its outward journey by Ivatt Class 2MT 2-6-2T No. **41286**, a Sutton Oak (8G) engine. First port of call was Vulcan Halt (p.u). Warrington B.Q was the next pick up point before a slight diversion via Walton Old and Acton Grange Junctions allowed main line running to Hartford Junction where the CLC was accessed. The Middlewich branch was then traversed, enabling reversal to take place at Sandbach, and as recorded here, a photo and water stop was taken at Middlewich itself on the return journey. From Northwich, a 'spirited' run was recorded as the special travelled east to Skelton Junction. Reversal on to the Timperley - Garston line allowed a further water stop at Warrington Arpley before going forward to Ditton Junction. Another reversal saw the train head for St Helens via Farnworth & Bold and Clock Face. Yet another reversal, for the final time, at Shaw Street, saw the intrepid party head for St Helens Junction and Earlestown, all for Twenty Three Shillings (£1.15p).
G Harrop courtesy A Haynes

(Left) **Middlewich, October 1956:** Rebuilt 'Patriot' No. **45540** *Sir Robert Turnbull* coasts into the station with an Up diverted express from Manchester. Signalman George Farrell holds up the miniature token for the section to Sandbach, which has only recently replaced a large metal trainstaff. To the right, the trellis work of the prize winning garden, lovingly tended by Signalman Jock Myles, is just visible. *T K Widd*

Middlewich Station

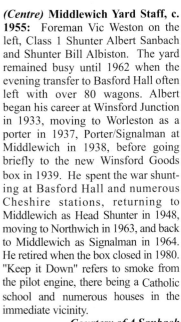

(Centre) **Middlewich Yard Staff, c. 1955:** Foreman Vic Weston on the left, Class 1 Shunter Albert Sanbach and Shunter Bill Albiston. The yard remained busy until 1962 when the evening transfer to Basford Hall often left with over 80 wagons. Albert began his career at Winsford Junction in 1933, moving to Worleston as a porter in 1937, Porter/Signalman at Middlewich in 1938, before going briefly to the new Winsford Goods box in 1939. He spent the war shunting at Basford Hall and numerous Cheshire stations, returning to Middlewich as Head Shunter in 1948, moving to Northwich in 1963, and back to Middlewich as Signalman in 1964. He retired when the box closed in 1980. "Keep it Down" refers to smoke from the pilot engine, there being a Catholic school and numerous houses in the immediate vicinity. ***Courtesy of A Sanbach***

(Left) **Middlewich, c. 1953:** No **41320** departs with the 1630 Crewe - Northwich as No. **44456** waits to help make up the 2000 to Basford Hall, the 'regulars' No's 41229 and 44155 being absent on this occasion. The Middlewich Pilot was a Crewe South duty, for many years the preserve of '3F' No. 3704, although 'USA' 2-8-0's were not unknown during the war. From 1950 Northwich shed initially provided a GC 'J11', much appreciated by the Middlewich based LNW drivers George Burrows, Ernie Worrall and Vic Woodward, but the turn was soon monopolised by '4F' No. 44155 until it disappeared following the closure of the ICI Works in 1962. *N R Knight*

(Right) Middlewich, 30th January 1965: Clearly aiming for an early finish, 'WD' 2-8-0 No. **90556** and her crew storm away on a fine Saturday afternoon with the 1029 Trentham - Shotwick Sidings coal. This traffic to Shotton steelworks was very heavy at this time and quite often double headed. The three high level sidings on the right would have been full before 1962 with Covhops and HG's for the Middlewich chemical traffic, but now store box vans for Northwich.

(Centre) Middlewich, 29th April 1967: No. **48531** heads a Grange Jct - Shotwick coal haul as No. **48551** on the 0840 Northwich - Crewe transfers shunts the yard which closed on 27th November. Until the closure of the ICI works in 1962, the yard also had its own trip working from Basford Hall and until the late 'Fifties handled much traffic for a wide agricultural area. Four coal merchants were served, ... *continued below*

.... and salt from Seddon's canalside works was delivered by white shire horses. Pochins Ltd. provided heavy timber traffic and in pre-war years milk and silk traffic was handled, the annual Middlewich show providing much livestock variety, including an elephant on one occasion!

Middlewich, April 1965: No. **41229** on the 1924 Northwich - Crewe parcels waits for No. **92022** to clear from Sandbach with the 1726 Heath Junction - Birkenhead coal. The station house - a fine example of LNWR domestic architecture - can be glimpsed above the parcels van. Next to the bridge is the original signalbox dating from the introduction of Block Working following an accident in thick fog at Croxton in 1881 when a passenger train collided with the preceding goods service. The porter's trolleys indicate that worthwhile parcels and pigeon traffic was still being handled. *Alan Wilkinson (3)*

(Above-left) **'Porter Jim' Lycett:** No account of Middlewich station could ignore this popular local personality who was Porter Signalman from 1935 until he retired in 1955. Jim started as a Junior Porter at Winsford Goods in 1905, moving to Over and Wharton as a Temporary Signalman, then to Parsley Hay before a 24 year stint as Porter at Hartford. Active in NUR circles, he also gave 50 years service to the St John Ambulance Brigade in whose uniform he is pictured, wearing the LMS Gold Ambulance Medal and other awards. Coming from a railway family, and always ready with a huge fund of stories he had no difficulty in pacifying your author in between trains!

A Wilkinson Collection

Nocturne, October 1964: An atmospheric scene as Jock Myles chats to the crew of No. **41229** with the evening Northwich - Crewe parcels, waiting for a Pilotman to Sandbach during a Block failure. The axle counters of the track circuit block introduced in 1960 with the new Sandbach power box were by no means infallible! Inside the box, the miniature token instrument for Northwich and token pouches are clearly seen. Jock, a talented gardener and model maker, was also paid to run trains which had the temerity to interrupt much more important business!

A Wilkinson

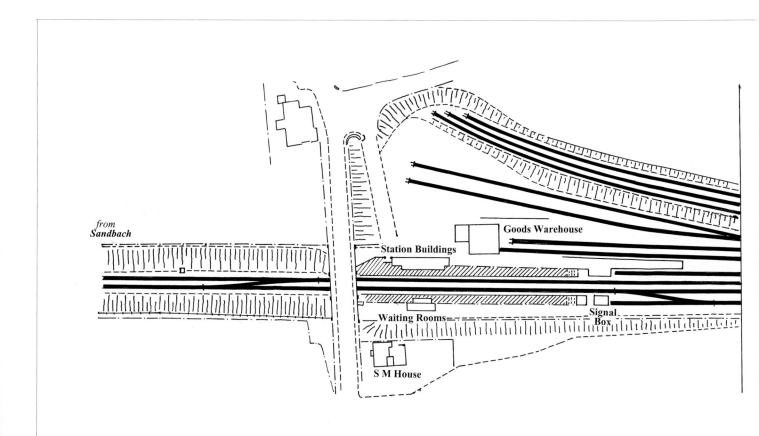

from **Sandbach**

Station Buildings

Goods Warehouse

Waiting Rooms

Signal Box

S M House

Middlewich, 3rd July 1964: '4F' No. **44079** eases the 0825 Silverdale - Northwich coal into Middlewich, when the long reign of the 'Stoke Scots' which had lasted since the replacement of North Staffordshire Railway locomotives on these workings in the 1920s, was rapidly drawing to a close. On the skyline, the ICI works is being dismantled, but Seddons and Murgatroyds works alongside are still in business, but alas not by rail. On the right is the site of the Mid Cheshire Alkali Works, rail connected by ground frame in 1888. The siding was disused by 1898, but was then used until 1962 to store empties for ICI.

A Wilkinson

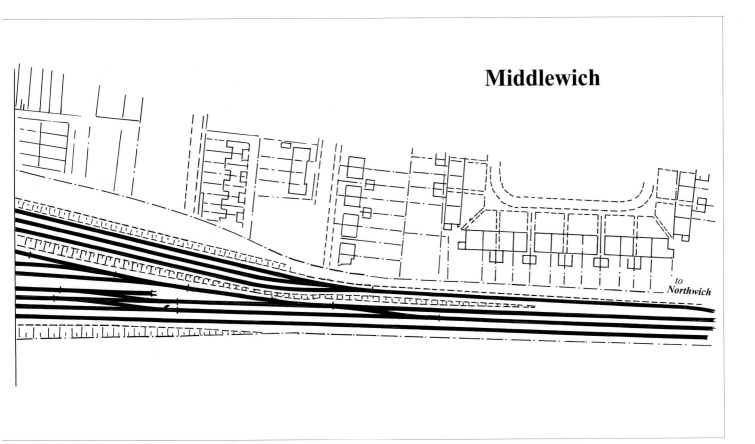

Middlewich

to Northwich

'Industrials'

ICI Works, Middlewich, c. 1935: All ICI's Mid Cheshire Works were shunted by diminutive Borrows well tanks. *Dalton* and *Moulton* arrived from Kerr Stuart & Co. in 1929. *Moulton* was scrapped in 1957, whilst *Dalton* went to Winnington in 1952, being replaced by another Kerr Stuart, *Priestly* of 1912. Diesel power in the form of a Ruston Hornsby 0-4-0 *Ramsay* arrived in 1956. *Dalton* is seen in the Mid 'Thirties; Northwich crews endured many vicissitudes when transferring such 'mini powers' between works over main line tracks!

I R S - Robinson Collection

Middlewich Salt Company

(Left-centre) Middlewich Salt Company, c. 1935: Verdin Cooke & Co's Bowfield Salt Works was connected by ground frame in 1903, and by 1919 the salt siding had been extended from Middlewich to H N Morris & Co's Tetton Salt Works nearby. These concerns later formed the Middlewich Salt Co. which provided at least one full train per day by the late 'Thirties. Pictured is Kerr Stuart 0-4-0ST *Witch* new in 1929, which had Hunset 0-4-0ST *Silkstone* of 1889 as a companion, both being scrapped in 1959 when a diesel arrived. Behind the engine are the distinctive gable roofed wagons which latterly operated in the yellow livery of the Cerebos Salt Co. In 1966, the new British Salt factory opened nearby and is now connected to the branch by a ground frame which replaced the salt siding in May 1979.

I R S - Robinson Collection

Murgatroyd's

Murgatroyd's New Works, 29th July 1960: This works opened alongside the line, one mile from Sandbach in 1949 became the home of immaculately kept Peckett 0-4-0 ST *Cordie*, delivered new to Murgatroyd's original salt works at Middlewich in 1940. Duties were shared with a Hunslet 0-6-0 ST *Anzac* from 1949 to 1959, but the inevitable diesel arrived in 1966 and *Cordie* was scrapped in March 1967. **D L Chatfield**

Cledford Bridge, 7th July 1965: '9F' No. **92165** tops the 1 in 132 out of Middlewich in fine form with the heavy 1630 Stanlow - Cliff Vale tanks carrying fuel oil for the modern kilns of the Potteries. Behind the train is the site of Cledford Bridge Halt - a 60 foot long wooden platform opened in 1911 to serve the nearby works of the General Electrolytic Parent Co., and Messrs Verdin Cooke & Co. The course of the siding to the GEP Co., installed in 1899, may be seen on the left. The company, later Electro Bleach and By Products Ltd., was absorbed by Brunner Mond & Co. and closed in 1928. The halt closed on 2nd March 1942. *A Wilkinson*

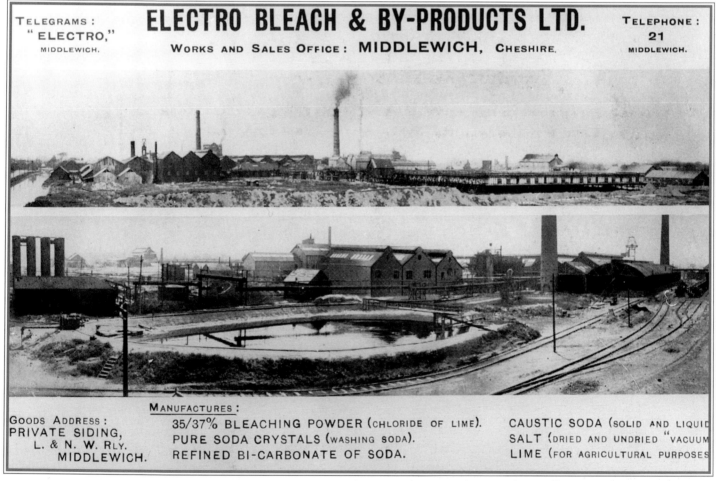

Electro Bleach Works, Cledford Bridge c. 1920: The opening of the Electro Branch factory in 1899 saw the salt siding extended to this works which had only a short life of 29 years. In the upper photograph, the Trent and Mersey Canal is on the left, and the railway out of sight on the extreme right. The works housed three 0-4-0 tanks. Peckett *Magneto* arrived in 1899, another Peckett *Magadi* came from the Ministry of Munitions at Marston about 1918, and Manning Wardle *Electro* was here for the duration, all being sold for further service when the works closed. *B S Jeuda Collection*

Seddon's Loading Bay, c. 1948: Lump salt is being loaded into covered vans and coarse salt being shovelled into ten ton, standard five plank wagons - clearly a labour intensive business. The narrow gauge hopper system extended throughout the salt works and across Brooks Lane to a wharf on the Trent and Mersey Canal. Seddon's wagon shop is immediately behind the photographer, whilst the remains of the loading bay canopy survived into 1993! *Seddon Collection - Northwich Salt Museum*

SEDDON'S SALT, MIDDLEWICH SALT COMPANY LTD., MIDDLEWICH (10 TON BOX WAGON FOR CONVEYING SALT)

For Captain Maurice F. Seddon of Datchet, Bucks.
This vehicle was built by the North Staffordshire Wagon Co. Ltd. and registered by the L.N.W.R. Co. It was fitted with brakes at both sides of the chassis, split type oil axleboxes and open type spoked wheels. As the photograph shows, the end stanchions of the vehicle were not fitted with strapping.
Livery: body and solebars were red oxide. The white lettering had black shading. The roof was covered with canvas which was painted black. All ironwork, with the exception of diagonal strapping, was black. Load: 10 tons. Tare: 7-7-0.

MAIN DIMENSIONS

Length over headstocks: 16 ft. 0 in.
Width over headstocks: 7 ft. 11 in.
Total height (rail level to inside of roof at centre of vehicle): 11 ft. 6 in.
Wheelbase: 10 ft. 0 in.
Plank widths: each plank was 8⅞ in. wide.
The small lettering reads: " 1. Empty to Middlewich Salt Co. Ltd. 2. Non-pool. Salt only."
The photograph was taken at Bristol Temple Meads in 1955 by J. H. Otto of Egmond-Aan-Zee, Netherlands, by whose kind permission it is reproduced.

(Below) **Seddon's Newtonia Works, c. 1948.** An interesting collection of box vans in Seddon's /Simpsons loading bay. Next to the LMS van appear to be three Simpson's vans, some with gable roofs, the four standard ten ton wagons for common salt. Three Seddon's covered vans in their distinctive red oxide livery complete the picture. *Seddon Collection - Northwich Salt Museum*

Seddon's - Salt - Middlewich

Approaching **Sandbach, 29th July 1960:** Longsight's 'Britannia' No. **70004** *William Shakespeare* runs under the newly erected Catenary and is about to run off the branch onto the main line with the up 'Pines Express' from Manchester to Bournemouth. This was one of several Manchester expresses diverted daily from 1957 - 60 during the Crewe - Manchester electrification. With freight traffic building up as well, the line was enjoying its busiest period. ***D L Chatfield***

Sandbach, 28th July 1960: Stanier 2-6-0 No. **42956** heads for Murgatroyd's new works with the Sandbach trip working. Previously, the line on which the 2-6-0 was running was a siding to Murgatroyds, but had become part of the Down approach to the Middlewich branch following electrification and the opening of the Sandbach power box in the background. The trip also served the salt works of Palmer Mann & Co., and the British Soda Co. at Rookery Bridge, and the goods depot at Ettiley Heath on the North Stafford branch. ***D L Chatfield***

Sandbach, 21st March 1957. A pre-electrification scene of the Manchester to Crewe line is encapsulated here in this view of Stanier Class 5 No **45289**, a Crewe North (5A) engine of long standing, passing alongside the Up platform with a short southbound passenger working. The left hand signal is 'off' for the passage of a train onto the Middlewich branch.

H Townley

Sandbach

Sandbach, 19th June 1952: No. **41229** heads the 1630 Crewe - Northwich 'Dodger'. The island platform was installed for the use of Northwich trains from 1888, and until about 1950 several workings reversed here rather than at Crewe. At this point No. 41229 was just $3\frac{1}{2}$ years old and had yet to receive her first repaint. *W T Stubbs Collection*